Essential Oils in Animal Care

A NATUROPATHIC APPROACH

Sarah Reagan, Kim Bloomer, & Jeanette Thomason

Willow Oak Publishing

Knoxville, TN

Spikenard (Nardostachys jatamans) is one of the most precious oils of ancient times. It is known as a spiritual oil. Biblical history indicates it was one of the last oils that Mary of Bethany used to anoint Jesus' feet at the Last Supper
(Image source: Wikipedia, public domain).

Copyright Notice

Copyright © 2014 by Sarah Reagan, Kim Bloomer, & Jeanette Thomason.

All rights reserved. No part of this publication may be reproduced, distributed or transmitted in any form or by any means, including photocopying, recording, or other electronic or mechanical methods, without the prior written permission of the publisher, except in the case of brief quotations embodied in critical reviews and certain other noncommercial uses permitted by copyright law. For permission requests, write to or email the publisher, addressed "Attention: Permissions Coordinator," at the address below.

Willow Oak Publishing
3600 Woodlawn School Road
Knoxville, TN/37920
Email: slreagan55@gmail.com

Bulk Ordering Information:
Contact Publisher at the address above.

All photos associated with this book are the property of one or more authors, or have been downloaded under common or subscription license agreement. If further information is required, please write to Publisher at the address given. Front book cover quote: A.A. Milne, 1882-1956.

Essential Oils in Animal Care: A Naturopathic Approach/ Sarah Reagan, et.al. —1st Ed.
ISBN:-13:978-0-9887222-3-1

Important Disclaimer Notice

The information contained in this book is intended for educational purposes only. The statements and products mentioned are not meant to diagnose, prescribe, treat, or cure any illness, disease, or injured condition of any animal (or human); furthermore, nothing in this book is intended to replace the advice of your veterinarian. Statements in this book have not been evaluated by the US Food and Drug Administration (FDA).

The authors of this book are not licensed veterinarians or other medical professionals and do not represent themselves as such.

Every effort has been made toward accuracy of the information provided. No one associated with this book, including the authors, the American Council of Animal Naturopathy, or its board members take responsibility for any results – positive, negative, or otherwise – that may occur from reliance on the information contained within this book.

Dedication

This book is dedicated to all the animals who have shared our lives before, those that do now, and will in the time to come. You have taught us much, and we look forward with anticipation to a continued journey of learning. There will never be appropriate words that can truly express the love and gratitude we feel and you are the reason we do this. Thank you.

Contents

Approaching Holism 1

The Eight Laws of Health 5

    Nutrition 5

    Exercise 6

    Water 6

    Sun & Supplements 6

    Temperance 6

    Air 6

    Rest 7

    Trust 7

What are Essential Oils & How do they Work? 9

    Good Vibrations 14

    There's Something in the Air 16

    Importance of Quality 20

    Have no Fear 21

How to Use Essential Oils with Animals 25

    Dosage 26

    Safe Use of Essential Oils with Animals 28

    Delivery Methods 32

    Putting the Oils into Action 41

Materia Medica 51

The Future of Animal Aromatherapy 61

Recommended Resources 63

Animal Chakra Charts 65

Frequencies of Essential Oils 67

Bibliography 69

Authors 71

Foreword

Maybe you are like I was, somewhere in between a little confused to completely in the dark on how best to take care of your pets. The truth is you have every right to be confused. Conventional "health care" for humans is the antithesis of health, and the world of "health care" for animals is also an absolute oxymoron. Today is the day that ends for you. This book will fully equip you to raise your animals properly and empower you to address all first aid needs at home with safe and effective Essential Oils saving you lots of money.

Upon graduation of high school and a lifetime of competitive hockey I thought I knew everything there was to know about health. The everything to know about health encyclopedia of my mind included protein, carbohydrates, fats, vaccines, annual check-ups, exercise, food guides and when in doubt call your doctor for a magic pill and a hammer to the knee. Then one day someone came along and lifted the fog for me, which began a quest of 10's of thousands of hours of real health research, a featured expert appearance in a Cancer documentary, and a North American speaking tour dispelling health myths, teaching first principles and eliminating the fear from Cancer.

Today is an exciting day for you because today is the day that someone is going to lift the fog for you when it comes to the truth about proper pet health care and save you a lot of money on vet bills! Today is also an exciting day for all pets of the present and future who will not have to suffer with the multitude of ailments in existence and have their lifespans cut in half any longer. Our pets are often some of our greatest friends on this journey we call life and losing them prematurely is both tragic and traumatic for pet owners and their families and it doesn't have to be this way.

It is my firm belief that you are about to learn from the foremost experts on proper animal health care. Not only do they have huge hearts for animals, but I can say with absolute certainty that they are teaching from proper first principles, offering species appropriate advice and most importantly they truly grasp the concept of holism and not the band aid/symptom based approach so commonly practised even amongst the "Natural Health Community". Kim Bloomer, CVND, ND, Jeannie Thomason, CVND, and Sarah Reagan, CVND and their team at the American Council of Animal Naturopathy are literally THE best place you could ever turn to for advice on rearing and healing your furry friends.

When it comes to health, objectivity for me is everything and having had the privilege of interviewing Dr. Kim Bloomer on several occasions and coming to know her personally I can assure you, she "gets it" like so few ever do. Having worked with many health professionals from every discipline imaginable I have always noticed they tend to get stuck in "Silo's" of information, schools of thought, blinded by emotions on issues and these things prevent people from being truly objective and sometimes even endorsing harmful practices in the name of being politically correct or "Integrative". To me the word integrative is a major oxymoron, you either believe in the laws of natural health or you don't. You cannot simultaneously believe in nature/natural laws and that poison is OK some of the time and these authors are very clear on this, which is rare and why they will serve you in the best possible way.

I think readers of this book will be so relieved to see the multitude of ways they can take care of their pets. You will no longer have to harm your pets and you will save a tonne of money on vet bills because you will now be empowered to use Essential Oils to address first aid concerns rather than turning to poison, which is sadly the standard when it comes to veterinarians.

I would like to finish by giving you, the reader, a huge congratulations for deciding to empower yourself and choosing to be just as loving and loyal to your pets as they are to you. And to the authors of this book thank you very much for the honour and privilege it is to be asked to write the foreword to this most excellent book! I am grateful for all the hard work that went into taking on the challenge of this book and very happy to see a credible book out that I can share with friends and family that teaches proper natural health laws and safe, effective use of Essential Oils with our furry friends.

Terry Tillaart
Mississauga, Ontario, Canada
7 July 2014

"Hence we conceive of the individual animal as a small world, existing for its own sake, by its own means. Every creature is its own reason to be. All its parts have a direct effect on one another, a relationship to one another, thereby constantly renewing the circle of life; thus we are justified in considering every animal physiologically perfect. Viewed from within, no part of the animal is a useless or arbitrary product of the formative impulse (as so often thought)."

—Johann Wolfgang von Goethe, 1749-1832 (Goethe, the Collected Works: Scientific Studies, p121; edited & translated by Douglas Miller, 1994)

Cypress (Cupressus sempervirens)

    Not to be confused with Blue Cypress (a different species), this species of Cypress is known as Mediterranean cypress and is native to the eastern part of that region. It is a long-lived, medium sized coniferous evergreen growing to about 115 feet tall, yet its roots reach deep into the earth, indicative of its "grounding" and emotionally stabilizing properties. It is believed that conifer trees were among the earliest essential oil bearing plants. Cypress oil has a very long history in humanity, being used in a number of traditional medicines. According to company information, Young Living distills the branches to obtain its Cypress essential oil. The interesting aspect of distilling Cypress is the time. Again according to company information, Cypress contains 280 constituents; if the oil is distilled for any time less than 24 hours (at low pressure and temperature), not all of the constituents will pass into the oil as the passage is only completed within the last 20 minutes of distillation. If the oil is distilled for longer than 24 hours, the chemical constituents are lost.

CHAPTER 1

Approaching Holism

Healthful Living embraces the principles of holistic or naturopathic health and healing for all living things. This paradigm philosophy and approach to well-being applies to true restoring health of body, mind, and spirit to their inherent design and purpose. About the year 400 BC, Plato said:

"The cure of the part should not be attempted without the cure of the whole. No attempt should be made to cure the body without the soul and if the head and the body are to be healthy, you must begin by curing the mind. That is the first thing. Let no one persuade you to cure the head until he has first given you his soul to be cured. For this is the great error of our day in the treatment of the human body, that physicians first separate the soul from the body."

Holistic health is not intended to serve as a Band-Aid or a one-time fix to a symptom. It is an ongoing lifestyle, a journey; ultimately it means living better and being healthier both physically and mentally.

Formulating a successful holistic lifestyle plan to keep our animals healthy relies on more than simply striving to keep them free of disease; it also involves maintaining a balance between each interdependent function of the body to reward optimum health.

Health from a perspective of holism is based on the principles that the body has the inherent ability to heal itself. Every illness has a cause – whether it manifests at the physical, mental, or emotional level – and symptoms are expressions of the body's attempt to heal. Symptoms are not the cause of illness, but if they are allowed to continue long enough, they may trigger other maladies and you can find yourself allegorically "chasing your tail" much as your dog might! The emphasis is on using the laws of nature to build health and prevent disease. True holistic health recognizes the "whole", but it also recognizes there are parts to the whole. These "parts" cannot be summed to make the whole, nor are the parts in summation "greater than the whole"; but each one *separately reflects the whole* – in other words each part is a hologram of the whole. Holism is a concept that the whole is reflected in each of the parts; one cannot cut away any part without reducing the entirety, yet we cannot conceive of the whole without going into the parts. (Bortoft 1996, pp4-18) And this is the connection, the relationship between whole and parts that the perspective of "conventional" vs "natural" fails to understand. What do we mean by "parts" or "reductionist"? We mean, for instance, analyzing the oils by their separate compounds without consideration of any synergistic effect from the combinations of those compounds as found in nature. We mean defining a symptom or set of symptoms as a "disease" without consideration of the basic underlying etiology. And so on. This is an extremely important concept and a differentiation from the mainstream "alternative" or "natural" health paradigm. To that end, we can embrace and understand reductionist science (the parts) without letting it become all consuming.

The authors of this book stand apart in these respects from the paradigms of both conventional "health" (which term is basically an oxymoron) and that of the current version of so-called natural health, which basically only gives lip-service to the laws of nature. The dichotomy of conventional vs natural health is a false one, and one cannot integrate something that is false. The truth lies within a science of holism.

It is with this understanding that we present this book. The use of essential oils (and supplements which we will not cover in this book) alone are not a "fix-all". They can, however, greatly assist the body in healing on all levels and can act as a sort of protective "armoring" against the increasingly toxic world we live in. It is important to also understand that using anything less than a clean, unadulterated, therapeutic grade essential oil will not only potentially be ineffective (translates into a waste of your money) – there is the real potential for physiological harm to any animal (or human for that matter). If we are trying to help an animal heal from the effects of toxicity, it certainly makes no sense to use a substance that is potentially toxic itself!

Every single essential oil mentioned in this book is based strictly on those obtained from Young Living. The authors of this book have used these oils collectively for many years and we each are confident on the quality sourcing of the oils. (See ordering information at end of this book.)

We have written this book with the objective of creating a handy, useful guide for using essential oils with our animals. To that end, we cannot address specific situations. We want to help instill in you – the animal's caregiver – a confidence of using these oils. There are many situations where conventional care has been averted with a working knowledge of essential oil use. The layout of the book flows from an overview of the underlying basics of health to defining what a therapeutic grade essential oil is, to a working description of some of the oils and their uses. We also wish to instill upon the reader the concept that all of life is integrated; animals are not separate from their environment – and that includes our influence upon them.

For those who wish to go beyond what information this book can provide, please inquire with the American Council of Animal Naturopathy (ACAN) about more in-depth courses in holistic health care for all common species of domestic animals.

Helichrysum italicum

The name Helichrysum is derived from the Greek words *"helios"*, meaning sun, and *"chrysos"*, meaning gold. It is a small perennial shrubby herb with narrow, silver-hairy leaves and small, yellow dry (straw -like) flowers. Also known as *Immortelle* and *Everlasting*, information on the historical use of Helichrysum is rather scant with it seemingly being used in both traditional herbal medicine and culinary use since ancient Greek times. Helichrysum is a relative newcomer to the aromatherapy scene with most essential oil catalogs not even listing it until after the early 1980's, according to Kurt Schnaubelt.

> *"Its effects are so convincing that it has never met with any kind of criticism despite the absence of data on its effectiveness. Helichrysum oil demonstrates that anecdotal evidence can create a reality without the help of industrially sponsored science. Helichrysum is more predictable in its action than almost any other oil and is produced and sold by small enterprises that understand the needs of the aromatherapy market." (Medical Aromatherapy: Healing with Essential Oils, K. Schnaubelt, g. 240)*

The essential oil yield for Helichrysum is quite low which contributes to its price, although the therapeutic value of this oil greatly exceeds the effort it takes to extract it, making it well worth the cost. Young Living's Helichrysum has been grown under organic methods on the Mona, Utah farm. It is now being proven to be a more suitable crop for the organic farm in Guayaquil, Ecuador.

CHAPTER 2

The Eight Laws of Health

Health does not depend on chance; it is a result of obedience to the laws of nature. All of creation follows natural law. The stars in their orbit, the birds that migrate in the winter, and the caterpillar that turns into a butterfly, the daffodils appearing in the spring – all follow these natural laws. The living body has been created with natural laws too.

In nature laws are not optional, if broken then consequences are certain to follow; one cannot run from or ignore the laws that are inherent and laid down in nature without repercussions.

Nutrition

Nutrition is the cornerstone. All species MUST eat what they were designed to eat in order to thrive. In nature, food is not cooked. It is raw and readily bio-available according to each species' unique anatomy and physiology. Dogs, cats, and ferrets are carnivores; horses are herbivores.

Processed foods are no better for animals than they are for people. Prior to convenience foods becoming widely available after World War II, dogs especially were commonly fed meat trimmings and raw bones; cats were many times allowed to forage for their own food. At that time, horses were already being fed some grain, mostly oats, perhaps some barley, but typically given a few times a day; they were still turned out to pasture at least during the winter. Not ideal for horses but certainly better than what we find the norm present day. With the advent of canned and bagged food and feeds, all the enzymes and nutrients went out the window along with truly nutritious ingredients. Dogs and cats both began to be fed processed, denatured food with fractionated, often synthetic, vitamins and minerals added back. Horses began to be restricted more from pasture and subjected to two meals per day (at most) of processed feed often times laced with processed sugars; again with "fake" vitamins and minerals added back to the bag to comply with minimum nutrition requirements. This shift from a more natural diet that relied upon the animal's innate knowledge to one designed in a laboratory by humans has led to allergies, skin disorders, digestive upsets and other health problems that have become far too common in animals today; a phenomenon which can be attributed to feeding non-species appropriate food, not to mention the use of chemicals in, on and around the animals. The old adage, 'you are what you eat', applies to animals as much if not more so than it does to humans. No quantity or quality of treatment – holistic or conventional – will have a lasting impact on the health of the animal if its diet is lacking in live nutrition. Therefore, balanced, *species appropriate* nutrition is the very first step to address when developing a holistic health lifestyle for your hairy, furred or feathered companions.

Exercise

Exercise is never optional. Animals were designed to move *daily*. In the wild foraging and hunting – depending on the species – is done daily. Movement is needed to find food, to grow and stay strong, to keep toxins moving out from the body.

Water

Always give pure, fresh, unadulterated water. Avoid water that treated with chlorine, fluoride or other toxins.

Sun & Supplements

Animals know what is needed to stay healthy. The nocturnal hedgehog, when sick, will go out in the sun during the day to help himself heal. Supplements are often times needed due to depletion of the soils which translates into nutrient-lacking food for herbivores which in turn translates into lack of nutrients in omnivores and carnivores. Supplements, however, should be from natural whole-food sources (not synthetic) and only used in moderation while qualified for each animal's unique needs. Supplements are also sometimes needed for those animals that have been vaccinated and on processed food/feed for some time, to help them transition to a species appropriate diet and lifestyle. We recommend you consult with a practitioner in these situations.

Temperance

Temperance is an old-fashioned word for moderation.

Air

Every living thing needs fresh air daily and, if possible, to be outdoors! Animals need to get outside to breathe in fresh air.

Rest

Animals need species appropriate rest without artificial lighting and all the noise of modern appliances and electronics that interfere with deep rest and bio-rhythms. Stress from improper rest can bring about illness and behavior problems.

Trust

Trust is not something we often think about as being a law of nature and health but there it is, as the eighth law. Trust is a firm belief in the reliability, truth, ability, and/or strength of something (or someone). As is always the case in nature, this law is multifaceted. First it means that we are to trust or have faith in the previous seven laws – nutrition, exercise, pure water, sunshine, temperance, fresh air, and rest – as being the true path to health, longevity and quality of life. Secondly it means to trust or have faith in the principles of naturopathy which are founded upon these laws of nature and health. To believe that these natural laws truly are laws and will always work. Trusting in the laws of health to the point of not becoming fearful when the body begins to detoxify or it appears to be taking longer to heal and then running back to conventional medicine. In reality, conventional medicine only masks or suppresses symptoms and never does allow healing or health to occur. And lastly, trust is building an honest relationship with the animals in our care rather than just making them do what we want; allowing for true companionship based upon mutual trust.

Myrtus communis

Common or "true" Myrtle should not be confused with another Young Living essential oil named Lemon Myrtle, the latter being a completely different botanical genus. Both oils are very effective in their own way; some of the healing properties may be similar but their chemistry is quite different. Myrtle is a native of the Mediterranean region; it is an evergreen shrub or small tree growing about 16 feet in height. While it does flower and produce berries that birds enjoy, it is the leaf of Myrtle that gives the most effective essential oil for healing purposes. As with many of the aromatic evergreens in their native regions, Myrtle is seen as a symbol of a strong life force. The use of myrtle as a plant has an ancient history and figures prominently in mythology, rituals, and ceremonies. Tablet IX, *The Story of the Flood* in the Epic of Gilgamesh mentions: "Seven and seven cult vessels I put in place, and (into the fire) underneath (or: into their bowls) I poured reeds, cedar, and myrtle." In Mediterranean antiquity it became known as the "plant of love", symbolizing beauty and youth, and was sacred to Aphrodite. These historical and mythical symbolizations of Myrtle can be seen in its present day properties of assisting in balancing many of the reproductive hormonal glands.

CHAPTER 3

What are Essential Oils & How do they Work?

Essential oils are the subtle, aromatic and volatile liquids extracted from the flowers, seeds, leaves, stems, bark and roots of herbs, bushes, shrubs, and trees, through distillation. According to ancient Egyptian hieroglyphics and Chinese manuscripts, priests and physicians were using essential oils thousands of years before Christ to heal the sick. They are the oldest form of remedies and cosmetics known to man and were considered more valuable than gold. There are 188+ references to oils in the Bible.

Essential oils work synergistically with the body to maintain, assist, repair, renew, etc., right down to the very DNA! While all plants principally have the capability of producing (and most do) essential oils, relatively very few produce enough to be worth the effort and expense to extract; this is not to say we may not "discover" more in time to come. Those plants that have aromatic qualities are the only ones that produce enough essential oil to use. (Balz *et al.* 1999, p27) It has been said that essential oils are "like the blood of the plant". Plants do not have "blood" – they do contain chlorophyll, which acts as a catalyst for photosynthesis. The interesting aspect, however, is that the color green is complementary to the color red and they are each the fluorescence of the other. (Balz *et al.* 1999, p15) So even though the function of volatile oils within plants is not the same as blood, it is inherently linked to the life force of mammals. The essential oils' purpose in plants is multifaceted, serving as both protection and communication – with each of these functions having a varying range of benefits depending upon the plant's needs. When properly extracted, these oils have the capability to translate those benefits into human and animal use. In a sense it is this variability and uniqueness that give a true essential oil its inherent power to heal; synthetic oils can never do this. Essential oils are volatile for a reason, allowing them to be carried spatially so their message can be communicated. The etheric forces of essential oils are outward radiating, allowing plants to communicate with each other while the fatty oils are inward focusing giving life preserving properties. (Stewart 2004, p704)

The term "essential oil" is a contraction of the original term, "quintessential oil". Ancient alchemical principles state the four elements of matter are earth, water, air, and fire. Aristotle determined a fifth element known as "spirit" or "life force". The term "spirits" remains in our modern day language to describe distilled alcoholic beverages; it is thought that ancient alchemical processes used some form of distillation/evaporation to remove and capture the "spirit" of the plant, producing this "quintessential oil". (Sell 2010)

There is a harmony that exists between plants and animals (including humans) that manifests itself in essential oils. In Anthroposophical terms, plants embody the etheric forces and the essential oils are their astralizing (or soul) element. Essential oils are both etheric and astral; they are both heating and cooling. Mary Hardy PhD says this:

"Essential oils heal the physical body by balancing the electrical frequency of the mineral (earth) aspect – minerals are electrically charged, and plants uptake minerals for their nourishment. The etheric body contains the chi (qi) or life force, it is the water element and since essential oils come from plants (which require water to live and grow – reaching toward the sun), by their very nature they will strengthen the lymph or immune system." (Hardy n.d.)

The morphology of the animal body can be viewed as three-fold, consisting of the rhythmic (respiratory & circulatory) system, the nerve-sense system, and the metabolic (including digestion) system. (Schad 1977, p30) An interesting analogy can be made between the different parts of plants (and therefore the essential oils that come from those parts) and the three-fold system. (Balz et al. 1999, pp15-17)

Plant		**Animal**
Flowers/fruits	⟵⟶	Metabolic system
Leaves/foliage	⟵⟶	Rhythmic system
Root system	⟵⟶	Nerve-sense system

We can see this, for example as nutmeg, distilled from the fruits and seeds, has protective gastric qualities as well as being an adrenal stimulant. Eucalyptus, distilled from the leaves, is well recognized for its expectorant and mucolytic properties.

Some of you may be familiar with homeopathy and the Law of Similars, as well as the concept of taking a vitamin or an herbal remedy to reverse a deficiency or excess in the body (the latter is actually referred to as the Law of Opposites which is as much a valid natural law as is the Law of Similars). Essential oils fall somewhat in that grey area between these two Laws. We can use them to "oppose" a high level of virus or fungi for example; this is their "physical" use. On an energetic or etheric level, we can also use them as "similars" to enhance a vibrational frequency (see the subchapter Good Vibrations). Much of the time, the oils are working in tandem within both the physical and the etheric realm. In any situation they should never be used as one-on-one replacements for allopathic drugs – this goes against the inherent purpose of these beautiful oils. As long as essential oils have been used in healing, they have been understood to have a balancing and strengthening effect upon the body, mind, and soul – and those principles of use remain the same today.

While the medicinal use of aromatic plants dates to the beginning of humanity, the modern term of "aromatherapy" did not come about until the 1920's – and the ensuing application within medicine was a decided shift from the intuitive, holistic understanding that existed previously (albeit at more of an unconscious level). The term, aromatherapy, was coined and put into practice by a French chemist named René-Maurice Gattefossé. This was the beginning of placing the use of essential oils (now called aromatherapy) into the realm of modern, reductionist science and sought to place the oils into the same contextual use as conventional pharmaceutical drugs. By the 1980's, essential oils had started to become a "natural" replacement for synthetic drugs, a practice some now place within the false concept of "integrative medicine".[1] Almost all of the modern research that has been done to date on essential oils breaks down the various compounds and attempts to isolate one or more "active components". From a practical standpoint, this materialistic research approach has advanced the mainstream use of essential oils, but it has also constrained their full inherent abilities to a large extent. As was discussed in Chapter 1, approaching phenomena from a "parts" perspective is not necessarily incorrect, and reductionism does not invalidate holism…if we understand that each part is a hologram of the whole.

> Like the ingredients of a chocolate cake…
>
> "Aromatic oil compounds do not act in isolation, which is why single compound studies are not a valid way to study the action of a whole, natural oil." (Stewart 2004, p312)
>
> [A major portion of the warnings against using oils containing ketones is based upon studies of isolated ketones administered in high doses to animals. (Stewart 2004, p336) Anything is lethal in high enough dosage.]

We hear people say all the time how there is clinical proof that the essential oils annihilate bacteria, fungi, viruses, etc., and make it so that they can't survive in the presence of the oils. If that were entirely true we'd all be dead because we have viruses, bacteria and fungi all around us and in us. We aren't "anti" any of these things as we understand how these microbes all play a vital role in life. We are FOR life. We are FOR health. We are FOR wellness. We are FOR

---

[1] The authors do not view "integrative medicine" as a valid concept, the full discussion of which is beyond the scope of this book; see Chapter 1 for a little more information on this.

healing. When the body is properly supported according to the LAWS of health mandated in nature by God, then it will thrive. Oxygenation is the primary energy metabolism of all cells in animals and humans; essential oils have the capability to enter through bacterial cell walls and interrupt this oxygenation and subsequent formation of ATP, interrupting the formation of pathogenic bacteria. (K. Husnu Can Baser, Gerhard Buchbauer 2010) In pleomorphic terms, the oils are changing the frequency of the microbes back to a healthy state, not "killing" off all microbes.[2] Since the oxygenation process is such a basic survival function of most life forms[3], the microbes do not develop resistance to essential oils as they do to conventional drugs (antibiotics, etc). (Verspoor and Decker 2000, p397) Essential oils have what we can call "homeostatic intelligence" (Stewart 2004, p379). Therapeutic grade essential oils have the capability to enhance, support, boost, and improve the body's own natural defenses so that it can heal itself. While those essential oils that have oxygenated compounds do not contain enough oxygen to actually deliver the element into the body (contrary to what some sources have indicated), by their homeostatic intelligence they can serve to both interrupt the cellular oxygenation process (as indicated above in dealing with pathogens), or they can enhance the process – it all depends on what the body needs at any given time.

Essential oils are not the same as herbal oils:
- ➢ Herbal infusions, when made in the traditional "digestive" method, use whole herbs processed under very low heat and are infused into fixed oils (vegetable oils).
- ➢ Essential oils are separations (distillations) of various plant constituents from the plant itself.

Essential oils are typically more powerful on a comparative volume basis than herbal oils if for no other reason than concentration of the sheer volume of plant matter that goes into the distillation process, but as we can and will see there are other reasons for the tremendous healing power of true therapeutic grade essential oils.

The chemistry of essential oils is very complex. Each one can contain a mixture of hundreds of compounds. There are two broad chemical groups found in essential oils: (Verspoor and Decker 2000), (Stewart 2004)

---

[2] Under the principles of pleomorphism, if there is too much of an overload (the definition of which is subjective from one organism to another) of, for instance, a particular kind of pathogenic bacteria, then there will be some amount of die-off as the population has to be lessened to facilitate healing. In part, this is why more severe "healing reactions" can occur in certain situations.

[3] Life forms living deep in the ocean that do not require oxygen have recently been discovered; as yet these life forms have not been found in mammals.

- Hydrocarbons:
  - Monoterpenes
  - Sesquiterpenes
  - Diterpenes
- Oxygenated compounds – some oils also contain oxygen:
  - Esters
  - Aldehydes
  - Alcohols
  - Phenols
  - Oxides

Terpene compounds are what allow a plant to be aromatic; they are especially found in the conifers. When the terpene compounds become oxygenated, they are called terpenoids.[4] It should be noted, however, that many sources use the term "terpenes" to include the oxygenated compounds. Mono- and Sesquiterpenes are the chief constituents of essential oils.

Our modern reductionist approach to science tends to isolate these compounds in attempt to determine which one(s) result in or cause certain reactions, and then attempt to duplicate them in isolation. Two major aspects are not understood by this approach: first of all, it is the synergism of the total compounds present that creates the healing power; secondly it is the human interaction and intent (the distillation procedure) with nature (the plant) that gives us these potent oils. No synthetic oil can ever achieve what natural essential oils can.

Essential oils affect not only physical healing but they can have a tremendous healing impact on emotions in a variety of ways. It has been demonstrated that essential oil molecules can pass the blood-brain barrier:

> "In June of 1994 the medical University of Berlin, Germany and Vienna, Austria discovered that … (sesquiterpenes) found in high levels in the essential oils Frankincense and Sandalwood will cross the blood-brain barrier. Sesquiterpenes … help to increase the oxygen in the limbic system of the brain which in turn "unlocks" the DNA and allows emotional baggage to be released from cellular memory. (This can help to change destructive behavior patterns – like binge eating or negative self-talk.)" (Verspoor and Decker 2000, p388) [quotes original]

Molecular size can be measured in AMUs, or atomic mass units. While it is not presently known for certain, it appears that molecules of less than 800-1000 AMUs are the only ones that can pass thru the blood-brain barrier. As well, most water soluble molecules cannot do so but lipids can. Essential oils, by nature of being volatile, have a molecular structure of 500 AMUs or less, with most being less than 300. They are also lipid soluble. These factors are what allow them to pass through the blood-brain barrier. (Stewart 2004, p449), (Stewart 2003)

The mind and emotions have a significant influence on the health of the physical body. Animals can certainly have emotional issues, just as humans do (in fact, in domesticated animals, most if not all of their emotional issues stem from ours). In naturopathy/holistic health it is recognized

---

[4] https://en.wikipedia.org/wiki/Terpene

that mind/emotions, spirit/soul and the physical body are not separate functioning entities or bodies. Essential oils are basically living energy that has the capability of affecting the flow of energy (communication) between the bodies. Some people feel a need to have definitive answers as to exactly what a particular oil can do within the physical body. Conventional science (chemistry) tells us the range of possibilities contained within the collection of compounds of any particular oil; no single oil can do everything (which is why blends may work better than singles in some situations). Quantum physics, on the other hand determines which of those possibilities actually happen – and those actions can vary at different times and in different individuals (animals)…again, within the established range of possibilities. When a human receives (or applies to an animal) an oil, the intent behind that action can guide the results of the oil (within the established chemistry). The oils themselves do not heal; they facilitate healing. It is the combination of chemistry, quantum physics, and intent that generates the healing process within body, mind, and spirit. So, when we apply or give oils to an animal, it is our intent that can affect the action of the oil. (Stewart 2009) We will get into the specifics of applying oils to animals in the "How To" chapter, and we certainly recommend utilizing some version of an essential oil desk reference (see Recommended Resources section) – but again, keep in mind that any kind of reference book is a guide to the range of possibilities.

Good Vibrations

Unfortunately most people nowadays do not have a concept of what a true state of health is – either for themselves or their animals; too many "disease" conditions have become accepted as the norm. It does not have to be that way. We have briefly discussed the importance of nutrition as the first of the eight fundamental laws of health – but it bears repeating and going a little deeper into this: <u>If the animal is not fed according to his/her biological requirements, you can expect health issues, sooner or later.</u> We have to begin there; no amount of essential oils can correct that aspect. A species proper diet translates into a proper functioning immune system which in turn translates into disease protection. Animals that are fed properly (and not vaccinated) do not attract disease and pests. Keep in mind that a good portion of the innate immune system is housed in the intestines. It also resides in the mucus membranes, lungs, lymph system, etc. The immune "system" is not a separate organ but is a composite of adaptable functions within and of the entire body, including the skin.

The body produces a finite amount of various enzymes; they must be replaced through food intake. If you are feeding your animal "dead" food (aka, processed, bagged, canned, etc), the enzymes will not be replenished.[5] Other enzymes in the body may take over, so to speak, for a while until they are depleted; this can lead to imbalance in gut flora, causing altered pH levels. This

---

[5] It is thought that pure, therapeutic grade essential oils can stimulate the body to produce enzymes. (Stewart (2011)

throws the immune system into overdrive as it tries to correct the various innate pH levels; bacteria begin to morph altering the native balance...eventually morphing into viruses or yeast. Those nagging episodes of allergies or bouts of diarrhea, cough, etc are the sign posts along the way of improper nutrition – they are not "bugs" that your animal "caught" that made him sick. As we approach the STOP sign, the body begins attacking itself, and voilà, your animal now has any of the various auto-immune "diseases". (Throw a few vaccinations in the mix and we can come up with cancerous tumors, seizures, or any number of other conditions.)

All animals are designed to eat a raw diet – yes, even herbivores. Since this is not a book on nutrition, we will not delve deeply into the subject, but suffice it to say: Dogs and cats need to eat raw, meaty bones; herbivores need to eat raw grass and herbages. This is the fundamental basis with which we need to work. As we saw above, plants depend upon electrically charged minerals for their nutrition.[6] If we can make the connection between mineral → plant → enzyme → animal, we can begin to see how frequency can be affected. In other words, substances[7] that originate as matter (the chemistry aspect) can function as energy (the quantum physics aspect). The concept of frequency with regard to health is easy to comprehend once we understand that plants use minerals as their nutrition source, and minerals, of course, have electrical frequencies. All animals, including humans, utilize plants in some way...even carnivores are indirectly dependent upon plants to provide the food of the prey animals they naturally seek to eat. It is by depleting the soil of minerals (and enzymes!) that we have depleted the nutritional value going into the plants that feed (directly or in-directly) our animals and us; and are thus decreasing the energetic frequency of the food supply that all of us depend upon. Unfortunately, we don't always have a choice of how our animals' food is grown or raised and we need to help them maintain a proper "vibrational level" to keep them healthy – this is where the use of essential oils can help tremendously.

Electrical charges are found everywhere, whether we detect them or not. That includes not just organic life but also includes inorganic minerals. D. Gary Young, Founder of Young Living, states: "Frequency is defined as a measurable rate of electrical energy flow that is constant between any two points." Dr. Robert O. Becker in The Body Electric established that the human body has an electrical frequency. Years prior to this, Dr. Royal Raymond Rife (1888-1971) established that diseases have electrical frequencies as well. Based on the research of both Dr. Rife and Dr. Otto Warburg, it was determined that a substance with a higher frequency will destroy a disease of a lower frequency. (Verspoor and Decker 2000, p389)

---

[6] Please note that enzymes play a vital role *in* the soil as well; the ability of plants to uptake minerals for nutrition is dependent upon healthy soil enzyme activity.

[7] Regarding essential oils, one of the primary "substances" (i.e. compounds) found is what is called the Aromatic Ring with benzene being the more prevalent one. These carbon rings basically have the capability to fluctuate between expressing themselves as matter and energetic waveforms; the energy is measured as frequencies, amplitudes, and phases. A full discussion of this is well beyond the scope of this book, but suffice it to say that there is an interchangeable relationship between matter and energy that has a pronounced effect upon all life. See the Recommended Resources section for information on linking to an excellent article by Dr. David Stewart on this.

Bruce Tainio of Tainio Technology built the first frequency monitor in the world. Tainio has determined that the average frequency of the human body during the daytime is 62-68 MHz; a healthy body frequency is 62-72 MHz. When frequency drops, the immune system is compromised. If the frequency drops to 58 MHz, cold and flu symptoms appear, at 55 MHz, symptoms of Candida overgrowth take hold, at 52 MHz, we see Epstein Bar and at 42 MHz, cancer. These frequencies should also apply to non-human mammals.

Since essential oils come from plants, we begin to understand how they can obtain their high frequency levels – if the plants are grown properly. The wonderful thing about medical grade essential oils is that they can help keep the body at the proper frequencies. According to Gary Young: "Measuring in [Mega]hertz, we found that processed/canned food had a zero [M]Hz frequency, fresh produce had up to 15 [M]Hz, dry herbs from 12-22 [M]Hz, and fresh herbs from 20-27 [M]Hz. Essential oils started at 52 [M]Hz and went as high as 320 [M]Hz, which is the frequency of rose oil. A healthy body, from head to foot, typically has a frequency ranging from 62 to 78 [M]Hz, while disease begins at 58 [M]Hz<. Clinical research shows that essential oils have the highest frequency of any natural substance known to man, creating an environment in which disease, bacteria, virus, fungus, etc., cannot live. I believe that the chemistry and frequencies of essential oils have the ability to help man maintain the optimal frequency to the extent that disease cannot exist."[8] [*Please note: all frequency measurements should be in MHz, not Hz.*][9]

There's Something in the Air

Atoms float all around us, unseen, with most of them having no real effect on us and our animals. However, normally one atom in every 100,000,000,000,000,000 is electrically charged – or ionized. That equates to about 1000-2000 per cubic centimeter, which is something equivalent to a handful of planets floating in a circle four billion miles in diameter. (Strachan and Karnstedt n.d.) You can imagine what would happen if all atoms carried an electrical charge…a rather electrifying experience![10]

Let's stop for a moment and briefly define what an ion is without getting too technical (and for those of you chemistry geeks out there, please forgive this extremely downsized version). Atoms start out as being neutral; they carry no electrical charge, having the same number of protons in the nucleus as there are electrons floating in orbit around the nucleus. Protons are the ponderous, positive, persevering guys that don't like to leave their nucleus home; the electrons are those easy-going, energetic, yet negative guys that go round and round in the atom's orbit, popping off here

---

[8] Again, as naturopaths we understand that it is not the objective to "kill" all microbes; the objective is to bring the body back into a state of homeostasis in which the microbes function as they are meant to.

[9] Corrections are from *The Frequencies of God's Voice and Those of Oils* by David Stewart, PhD; http://www.raindroptraining.com/messenger/v11n3.html#voice

[10] The discussion in this book about ions considers only the small ones, which apparently are the only ones to affect living matter. Soyka (1971, 1977)

and there to the neighbor's when the fancy strikes. When an electron moves in or out of an atom's orbit, that atom becomes electrically charged, either positive or negative and is no longer called an atom but is now called an ion. Since those energetic electron guys are the ones that move around, they (not the protons) determine whether an atom becomes a positive or negative ion (pos-ion or neg-ion). When an electron leaves one atomic home and moves into another one, that new atomic home (the one that gained an electron) becomes negatively charged and the old atomic home (the one that lost an electron) becomes positively charged.

So, what does all this mean for the living beings inhabiting Earth, and where do essential oils fit into all this? All matter is made up of atoms and their combinations – molecules; and that includes the air we breathe. Nature always tries to seek a balance…and as we saw above, the great majority of the atoms inhabiting air are balanced in their number of protons and electrons, meaning there is no electrical charge. But nature also likes to spice things up a bit now and then just so we can practice our homeostasis act. Enter the "maverick" molecule, or ion, to tilt that balance one way or the other. Nature provides us with events like thunderstorms and "witches winds" that can drastically increase the number of those positive guys. In a calm, typical open air atmosphere (technically, the troposphere is where we live), there is a ratio of about 5:4, pos-ions to neg-ions; and it is thought that is the balance or ratio in which life began and evolved. (Soyka 1971, 1977, p20) The Earth itself is negatively charged and thus can absorb or offset the positive charges from weather events that nature throws at us from time to time.[11] Nature has also given us wonderful places like the seashore, waterfalls, and forested areas in which the normal ion ratio is reversed, with neg-ions being markedly higher. That may be why we naturally seek these areas in which to "get away from it all". Dust in the air absorbs neg-ions, which is why we typically find more neg-ions in these areas with less atmospheric dust. (Soyka 1971, 1977, p24)

Human technology has given us wonderful devices such as computers (which you wouldn't be reading this book if it weren't for a computer), cell phones, microchips, and so on that all carry electrical charges. Unfortunately, these artificial devices have tipped the normal balance of pos-ion: neg-ion to a marked increase in favor of pos-ions. This has a negative health effect on the vast majority of people, animals and plants. Natural ions typically do not live long and the process in nature of forming ions is a continuous one; man-made environments have thwarted this natural occurrence and it becomes permanent. (Soyka 1971, 1977, pp25-26) This technology is obviously not going away, so we need to find ways to help re-establish nature's balance…and since therapeutic/medical grade essential oils produce negative ions, this is one obvious place to start.

Ions are closely involved with the oxygen process; plants create oxygen which could not happen without atmospheric ions. (Soyka 1971, 1977, p20) Ion research indicates that neg-ions can act upon the body's capacity to absorb and utilize oxygen, thus accelerating the delivery of oxygen

---

[11] Bare feet touching the Earth also help neutralize an animal's positive charges (as well as us). Animals that spend as much time outdoors as possible are healthier overall, with this "grounding" being one major aspect.

to cells and tissues. Evidence also supports theories that ions break down serotonin in the bloodstream. (Strachan and Karnstedt n.d.) Inhaling diffused essential oils that give off negative ions may be of benefit in all these ways.

Research has further shown that animals (and insects) can display "an explosion of energy" (i.e. what we may think of as hyperactivity in our animals) in the hours, even a couple of days, before an approaching storm or wind event. (Soyka 1971, 1977, p22) The more electrified the weather disturbance the greater the hyper behavior can be for the longer period of time prior. Many times we interpret this as a behavioral problem with the animal. Instead, understanding that their connection with nature is likely a better predictor of weather than the meteorologist, giving them an opportunity to inhale certain essential oils can help to at least reduce this stress (in both you and your animal!).

Even though atmospheric electricity has been a known phenomenon since the mid-1700s, the research on the effects of ions on living beings was not begun in earnest until the 1920s. It is a fascinating subject of which much is still not known. We invite you to read further on both the subject of ions as well as frequencies; please see the Recommended Resources section.

Ion Prisons

William Radley of Bio-Environmental Systems refers to the typical polluted American city as an "ion prison". All the pollution, not to mention the man-made building materials, act to absorb negative ions. Ion- counts can reach as low as 100/cubic centimeter, while the minimum amount for optimal human functioning is about 1000/ccm. (Strachan and Karnstedt n.d.)

Plants contribute to the negative ionization of air from the essential oils they release. (Balz et al. 1999, p14) Increasing the amount of plant and tree life in urban areas can help reverse the effects of these "ion prisons".

It is interesting to note that pos-ions slow the sweeping action of tiny hair-like cilia in the throat from 900 to 600 beats per minute and cut mucous flow, increasing susceptibility to airborne allergens. (Strachan and Karnstedt n.d.)

Importance of Quality

A therapeutic grade essential oil can be defined as one that is purposefully (and intent should not be disregarded here) distilled from plants that are either cultivated organically without pesticides or herbicides, or grown wild in a clean, non-toxic environment. It is important that the proper botanical genus, species, and cultivar are identified. They should also be extracted by steam distillation at low pressure/low temperatures without chemical solvents, and for the proper length of time to ensure no significant loss or exclusion of lighter or heavier chemical fractions. The vessels in which the distillation is done should absolutely be made of food grade, inert materials.[12] As you can readily see, getting an essential oil from plant to bottle is no small feat and requires thorough knowledge of the entire growing, harvesting, and distillation process. (Stewart 2004, p7)

At the present time, there are currently no organizations that regulate or certify "therapeutic grade" essential oils. There are at least a few companies that market their oils – including the Young Living company – as therapeutic grade. While the authors cannot speak for these other companies, we are confident in Young Living's trademark of "Young Living Therapeutic Grade Essential Oils™", and that the company's essential oils meet or exceed every definition of "therapeutic grade" as stated above. All YL oils meet, and most exceed, the minimum standards set by the two primary international standard-setting organizations. One of these organizations is known as the France-based Association Francaise de Normalization (AFNOR); the other is the Swiss-based International Standards Organization (ISO). Both of these organizations set standards for many products, not just essential oils; neither organization has any in-house capability to test essential oils. They only set standards as agreed upon by the industries involved; they do not certify quality. The typical standards from AFNOR/ISO usually consider minimum concentrations of only one to six ingredients that are of specific interest in a particular oil, and ignore all other constituents; their standards do not differentiate between naturally occurring compounds and synthetic ones. For example, if an oil contains enough menthol, you can legally sell it as "peppermint" when, in fact, there may be no actual peppermint oil from the plant present whatsoever. Hence, an aromatic oil can be 80-100% synthetic and meet AFNOR/ISO standards. Their compliance standards also do not designate testing for toxins such as herbicides, pesticides, etc, in the finished product; nor do they address the issue of high pressure/high temperature distillation used by some companies which effectively destroys the therapeutic constituents while leaving those of interest to satisfy the perfume industry.[13]

What is even more important, however, is that the YL company maintains very strict internal testing standards as well as submission to third-party labs and independent audits of their oils.

---

[12] Exceptions to the steam distillation are the citrus oils which are typically cold pressed.

[13] From an article by David Stewart, *The True Meaning of AFNOR*; http://www.raindroptraining.com/messenger/v3n3.html#true

The company currently has ten farms globally and is actively pursuing purchase of more land and/or farmer growing contracts. The farmers who grow for YL under contract are subjected to the same strict standards as applied to the company-owned farms; as well, the effort is made to teach the contract farmers proper organic growing techniques, an education that benefits them in many ways. The bottom line is that Young Living's own standards far exceed those of either AFNOR or ISO.

This book was not written to "sell" a particular brand of essential oil, but we emphatically feel it is imperative that the reader understands there can be extreme differences in quality between brands. Many essential oils are processed with harsh chemicals, diluted, or synthesized in a lab. Cheap copies not only lack the ability to generate healing they have the potential to be toxic. We personally use and recommend Young Living Essential Oils to our clients because they are tested and proven to be unadulterated, being the purest, medical/therapeutic-grade essential oils available in our opinions. The company's Seed to Seal® process sets the standard for purity and authenticity in modern essential oil production.[14] The company also maintains a standard of transparency by both making their test results available and through the several hands-on events held every year in which distributors can participate in planting, harvesting, and distilling activities, seeing first-hand the process that YL oils go through literally from seed to seal.

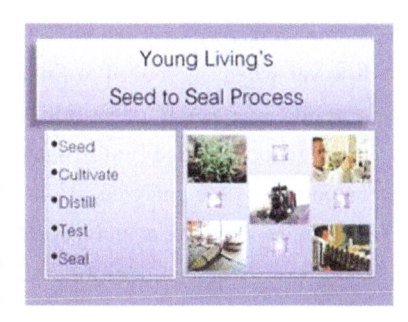

Have no Fear

When it comes to using essential oils with animals there are a few areas that tend to strike fear in people: there is a lot of misinformation about EOs being dangerous to use around animals, especially cats and birds; there is a certain amount of trepidation associated with not just what oils to use but when, how much, diluted or not, etc; and perhaps the biggest misnomer of all is qualification…"I'm not qualified" or "I don't know enough". As care-givers of animals, no matter what species, we all have a certain responsibility toward them, and this causes fear in many people because they have been led to believe that only "certain" people are capable of this kind of knowledge. This simply and emphatically is not true. With a little effort each and every person that cares for animals is capable of maintaining them in a thriving state of health…all that is necessary is a basic understanding of what species appropriate means and what each class of animal requires.

---

[14] You can read more about this process here:
http://www.youngliving.com/en_US/discover/quality

The issue with essential oils being dangerous to use around and with animals comes primarily from the British school of philosophy on essential oil use. There are primarily three "schools" of practical application of aromatherapy (or therapeutic use of essential oils). The British school emphasizes application via massage and almost always using diluted oils (dilution rate at about 95%+ most times); they discourage neat (undiluted) application of any oil. Interestingly, the British school of aromatherapy was begun by a French woman (Marguerite Maury) who was a biochemist and very familiar with the medical (internal) application of essential oils in France. However when she moved to England, because she was not a medical doctor, she felt she should focus on non-medical usages utilizing significant dilutions. Much of the warning data cited by the British school is based [unfortunately] upon animal studies, studies in which only single chemical components were analyzed, studies using non-therapeutic/perfume grade [i.e. adulterated] oils, and studies which related anecdotes of children accidentally drinking large amounts of essential oils or even women attempting to induce abortion by large doses of oils. (Stewart 2004, pp3-4, 484) [comments added]

The French school of aromatherapy emphasizes internal use of essential oils (although in practice all methods of application are utilized – see next section, How to Use Essential Oils); however it also treats essential oils as "natural" pharmaceutical replacements. The German school emphasizes inhalation as the best method of application. (Stewart 2004, pp3-4) The French and British schools seem to be the dominate philosophies practiced in the United States.

The authors of this book agree with both the French and German methods inasmuch as we know from experience with animals (and ourselves) that therapeutic grade essential oils can be used neat (with some exceptions); that they can be taken internally (again, with some exceptions); and that inhalation is an excellent delivery method. But the similarity ends there as we also approach all of health from within holism. We do not look upon the use of essential oils as 'natural drug replacements', but we do understand that essential oils can have a very pronounced effect upon not just the physical body, but mind and spirit as well. We understand that these therapeutic grade essential oils can communicate with the body on a cellular level. And we also understand, as stated previously, that the basis for all true animal health lies in a species appropriate diet.

The Maxim of Toxicology states:

"Dosage is everything. Everything is toxic. Everything is therapeutic. It all depends on dose." (Stewart 2004, p119)

Yes, even pure, unadulterated, therapeutic grade essential oils can become toxic if given in excess. This is not something to fear, it simply means a healthy dose of common sense and a little education goes a very long way! We will explore this in more detail in the "How to" chapter.

So, while we strongly recommend that in serious, complex situations you consult with a knowledgeable practitioner[15], there are many day-to-day situations in which the use of essential oils can benefit your animal. These situations include both acute/first aid types as well as helping with chronic issues…and not to mention general overall health; and if you are in consultation with a practitioner, this book will help guide you. When you apply or use these oils with your animal in a fearful or hesitant manner, you will not see the healing actions that you could when approaching the situation with confidence and conscious intent. This book is intended to help you overcome these fears and help you to gain confidence in using therapeutic grade essentials oils with your animal. And remember, if in doubt, ask and read.

For more information on the safety precautions when using essential oils with animals, please see the section Safe Use of Essential Oils.

---

[15] Certified Holistic/Naturopathic animal practitioners are listed on the website of the American Council of Animal Naturopathy – http://www.animalnaturopathy.org/

Palo Santo tree (Bursera graveolens)
(© 2008 - Patricia Jaramillo, Rachel Atkinson, Anne Guézou, Charles Darwin Foundation.
Licensed under Creative Commons)

Palo Santo is also known as "Saint Wood" or "Holy Wood". It is native to Mexico and the Yucatán Peninsula down to Central and South America including Costa Rica, El Salvador, Guatemala, Honduras, Colombia, Ecuador, and Peru. This species belongs in the same botanical family as Frankincense and Myrrh. It has historically been widely used in folk medicine with essential oil production attracting the most interest present-day. It was used by the Incas as a spiritual remedy for purifying and cleansing; local customs attributed the ability to remove "bad energy" to Palo Santo. In order to obtain a true therapeutic essential oil from Palo Santo, the cut wood must age (generally several years); freshly cut wood does not produce the same chemistry. This is why it is said that the spirit of the tree (or fallen branch, etc) imbues the essential oil with its healing powers. The trees are protected in most (if not all) areas of harvest and those who harvest the wood are allowed only to take the dead wood from fallen trees or broken limbs. According to company information, Young Living is currently re-planting the trees on the Young Living Ecuador farm.

CHAPTER 4

How to Use Essential Oils with Animals

Animals benefit from essential oils because they are a natural solution for many common physical or behavioral problems, whereas synthetic drugs can only palliate at best and many times drive symptoms deeper into the body. There is no such thing as a "mild" side effect for any conventional drug. As we saw earlier, essential oils serve plants in both communicative and protective ways. Just as essential oils can protect a cut in a tree from pathogens (and thus allow healing processes) they can help heal wounds in our animals. While essential oils do not chemically contain molecules of hormones, vitamins, proteins, or enzymes, they do carry the blueprint of all these molecules and compounds. (Stewart 2011) They also do not generally contain amino acids as they easily oxidize and disappear; the exception being that traces for amino acids have been found in cumin essential oil. (Stewart 2004, p140) This is where the communication part comes in; and as we saw earlier, the volatility of an essential oil is necessary to carry it – this blueprint. The messages from essential oils are carried internally just as any other internal cellular communication happens. The practical application of this can be, for instance, to regulate the hormonal cycle or to balance an excess or deficiency of hormone production.

Since essential oils are made of primarily non-metal elements, they typically carry a negative ionic charge. Oils containing certain compounds – acids, phenols, and esters - could become positively charged when placed in water; however generally have minor implications as the acids are weak and the therapeutic action of the oil will not suffer. Most essential oil compounds do not have an affinity with and thus will not ionize in water therefore they typically do not manifest either an acid or alkaline pH, remaining neutral.[16] What does happen when an oil is ingested is that natural acid in the body will destroy (or break down) the essential oil molecules thereby releasing their compounds, and thus the body receives the benefits of whatever compounds are in

---

[16] Stewart, D., 2004. *The chemistry of essential oils made simple: God's love manifest in molecules.* 1st ed. Marble Hill, Mo: Care Publications; statements confirmed via email 05/20/2014.

that particular oil or blend. (Stewart 2004, pp347-350) Again, this happens on a homeostatic basis – only if the body needs those particular compounds will it utilize them.

Animals typically have an incredibly keen sense of smell…much more than we humans do. But just as the oils do with us, when a dog, horse, cat or bird[17] smells an essential oil the molecules pass via his olfactory system to the limbic area of the brain (which is the area that deals with emotion, instinct and regulation of many of the body's systems); for instance the response that would tell the body to reduce inflammation. And being animals, we find that our furry/hairy (or feathered) companions tend to utilize inhalation in a more correct way, so to speak, than many of us humans do; again, because they are more dependent upon their acute sense of smell. This is why most times it is important to give an animal a chance to "tell you" whether the particular oil you have selected is right or not. It is also important to correctly interpret the animal's response to the oil. For instance some people may see a horse flare his nostrils at an oil and think he doesn't like the smell when, in fact, the horse is using his extremely sensitive olfactory organs to completely take the oil into the limbic system.

Animals remain very much a part of nature, seeming to have a natural affinity to the healing influence of the oils; they have a much greater innate sensory system and can be more sensitive to the effects of essential oils than humans. (Although humans certainly could be more intuitive about using essential oils if we would take a break from trying to dismember and quantify everything!) For instance you may have two or three oils that could work in a given situation. How to choose the correct one? Ask the animal!

Dosage

Regarding dosing of essential oils (singles and blends) in animals, some will recommend to dose by weight. However that may not be the most appropriate approach, especially with animals, but with humans as well. Using a typical human (average weight of 160) dosing protocol of 3-5

---

[17] There seems to be a long-standing, ongoing debate as to whether birds have a sense of smell or not. Recent research suggests they indeed do have olfactory capabilities.

drops, translating that into a dose for an animal as large as a draft horse at about 1600-2000+ pounds could lead you to dose over half of an entire 5 ml bottle at one time!

David Stewart says:

"A single drop of essential oil contains 40 quintillion molecules. ... You have 100 trillion cells in your body. Hence, one drop of oil is enough to cover every cell in your body with 400,000* molecules." (Stewart 2004, p483; *corrected via email dated 07/26/14)

Now you can see why one drop, or even just a whiff, of essential oil is capable of accomplishing the intent. It is the purpose of application around which the dosage of an essential oil should pivot…and this applies for any animal, human or not.

Cells in the body have receptor sites, like little doors with locks on the surface of each cell; and there can be thousands on each cell. These receptor sites are the communication portals of cells, and this is how substances (e.g. hormones, etc) get their messages into the cell; these substances communicate by vibrations or the electromagnetic properties, not mechanics. (Stewart 2004, pp228, 482-483) However these receptor sites can be overloaded. What happens in that situation is not unlike a telecom overload – too much data being transmitted at one time and nothing being understood as it was intended. Either nothing gets accomplished (the signals have been jammed) or something happens that wasn't really desired (oops, we have a misunderstanding). Essential oils also communicate their messages via receptor sites. So it stands to reason that if all you really want to do is whisper a message, a megaphone is not needed. Sometimes the body suffers trauma and there is a lot of activity going on (various inflammatory responses, etc). In those situations we may need to become a little bolder in our message. This can be accomplished by more frequent dosing instead of more quantity at one time. But never in any way should it be necessary to give more than 10 drops at any one given time to an animal, and in fact we recommend half that as a typical upper level dosage…yes, even for the 2000 pound draft horse; his cellular receptor sites are no less receptive than a 20 pound dog.

How will you know when to use less and when to use more? Practice mainly, as well as an understanding of the particular situation you are trying to address. If in doubt about that part, ask questions of those who you trust to be knowledgeable in that specific area. As for the amount of oil to begin with, when in doubt always start with less, you can increase as needed. Don't hesitate to let the animal guide you. Do not be afraid of the dosing part…you will not cause any harm by using three drops instead of two, or six instead of five.

Safe Use of Essential Oils with Animals

Based upon our experience as well as that of others, Young Living Essential oils are the only essential oils we recommend as pure enough to use with animals (and humans for that matter). As we discussed previously, much of the fear of using essential oils with animals comes from the practice philosophies of the British school of aromatherapy, which in turn are based upon studies of isolated chemical compounds or substances, not the entire oil. Many of these studies were done on animals who are generally more sensitive than human beings to begin with; and furthermore the oils from which the compounds were taken were, many times, those used to supply the perfume industry. A single natural substance can be given by itself and be deadly, but in synergy with the other constituents – and at the proper dose – of a complete natural oil, it is rendered safe. (Stewart 2004, pp21-24) Once again, there is a huge difference between pure, therapeutic grade essential oils and perfume grade or adulterated oils, the latter being not just potentially dangerous but void of healing properties.

Safety precautions of Young Living oils in use with animals will depend upon the method of delivery as well as the species. The overriding cautionary statement is to never force any essential oil in any method upon an animal that is showing obvious signs of rejection. There is a tendency to view the use of essential oils as a "natural" replacement for allopathic drugs, which leads us to become the sole authority in making decisions of what oil, when and how, the animal should receive. Animals have a tendency to know better what is good for them and what is not than we humans seem to.[18] Please allow them to communicate this. As for dilution, again this depends upon the particular oil (or oil blend), the animal species involved, as well as the purpose of application.

Regarding diffusion, please always have fresh air available and allow the animal to leave the room if desired. There are "clinical" times when you may want to "force" diffusion; again always allow for fresh air ventilation and never diffuse any oil more than 5 – 10 minutes at a time unless you know for a fact the animal can tolerate more (up to 20 minutes maximum). Observe the animal; if becoming restless, stop the diffusion. You can always do another diffusion session later. In voluntary inhalation methods of delivery (such as from the bottle or your hand), it would almost be impossible to cause an overdose unless you restrict the animal and force the dosing – we sincerely hope no one would ever do that. As for topically, you can cause some sensitivity reactions especially in a neat application of the "hotter" oils so we recommend always diluting those oils (see the section on Topical applications for more information). Common sense as well applies here – keep the topical application to a few drops, not half the bottle. And remember – essential oils

---

[18] The exception to that may be an animal that is quite ill or seriously hurt; there may be appropriate times to "force" an oil, but we highly recommend you only do so during consultation with a knowledgeable practitioner. We also recognize that an animal who has never experienced a species appropriate lifestyle, including diet, may have suppressed sensory mechanisms.

applied topically are diluted by fatty oils, not water (water intensifies the action of the oil). The only time you will need more quantity of oil based upon size of animal is when doing a whole body massage; obviously the larger the animal the more quantity of massage oil/EO mix you will need.

Aside from the caveats given above, internal consumption is really the only delivery method in which any serious overdosing can occur. And again, common sense applies here. Just because a horse weighs ten times more than a dog does not mean the horse should receive ten times more oil. Even an elephant would not need 50 times more oil than a ten pound dog. Essential oils are not food and are not "fed" by weight. If ever in doubt, less is the best approach; you can always add later but you can't immediately remove an oil given internally; it will have to digest.

As for giving a variety of oils at one time, that is going to depend upon the individual situation and again we recommend a healthy dose of common sense. We have already discussed the concept of receptor sites so it makes sense that you can "jam the signals" – or in this case confuse them – by not just too much quantity of oils but by too many oils at one time or in rapid succession. Young Living has some very good essential oil blends; look at those blends and the number of oils contained in them. Our recommendation would be to never exceed that number of single oils in one session and preferably keep it to less than six (the exception being a Raindrop Technique, which may typically be seven single oils). If you are using a blend, then you may want to wait a period of time before administering another oil be it a single or blend.

A summary of common sense precautions include:
- Never place essential oils (diluted or not) directly in the eye; it may be appropriate at times to lightly rub around the eye always keeping in mind that the vapors of strong oils can get in the eye; never force this.
- Never use undiluted essential oils in the ears and never pour them (even diluted) into the ear; always use an appropriate cotton swab to apply the diluted oil being careful to never penetrate deeply.
- Keep the oils themselves out of reach of animals (and children) at all times.
- Always keep a bottle of organic vegetable oil on hand to dilute the effects of using essential oils in a neat form if necessary.
- Pay attention to those oils that contain furanoid compounds as they can make the oil phototoxic (see note in the Materia Medica section).
- Some essential oils are contraindicated in situations of animals being seizure-prone or having high blood pressure (see note in the Materia Medica section).
- When using a water application such as foot soaking or bathing, always use a bit of a dispersant (such as two or three drops of Animal Scents shampoo) to eliminate any concentration of the essential oil gravitating to the body.

There are two species within the more common domestic animals that bear additional information regarding safe use guidelines.

Cats

Cats are known to be deficient in their ability to eliminate compounds through hepatic glucuronidation (they lack enzyme glucuronyl transferases). Glucuronidation is an important detoxification mechanism present in most animals except cats. Lack of this important detoxification mechanism in cats may result in slower elimination and thus possible buildup of the toxic metabolites in the body causing toxicity problems. When using oils with your cat, less is generally better, and this means less compared to any other species (except perhaps for birds). As indicated above, ensure good air circulation especially during the diffusion process, so that local concentrations of essential oil vapor are not built up in areas inhabited by the cat. Make sure the cat can get to undiffused air any time he wants to, and only diffuse in an individual room if the cat can leave the room or make it a multi-room location. Toxicology studies show that the feline liver usually needs 48 hours to process and excrete "terpenes", thus allow 48 hours between the end of the last diffusion and starting another to avoid repeated exposure by inhalation. Diffusion is generally the first (and easiest) recommended way to administer oils to cats.

Cats are much more fastidious than dogs; many if not most cats are not fond of anything that has a distinct odor being applied to their body, whether you think it smells good or not. Raindrop technique has been used successfully with cats; always dilute the essential oils with a carrier oil when applying Raindrop. Cats are not generally as fond of staying in one place for extended periods of time when being "messed with" as perhaps dogs are. Therefore, when doing a Raindrop technique with a cat, it may be much easier to pre-mix all the desired RDT oils into a dropper bottle with the carrier oil, and basically do a "combined" RDT instead of dripping the oils one at a time. Many cats enjoy being petted and this can be a good opportunity to apply either a single oil or two or a blend. To do a Petting technique with a cat, rub a drop or two of the desired oil(s) between your palms, allow it to dry, and "pet" lightly fluffing the coat instead of stroking it down. Even though the oil has dried, the cat will still be receiving the energetic healing benefits. If the oil bottle recommends dilution, please do so with cats even if you "ignore the rules" for yourself!

Some cats will tolerate – and some may enjoy – oils dosed internally. There is no reason to not give an oil internally in a neat form provided it is therapeutic grade (i.e. from Young Living). Cats have very high levels of stomach acid (assuming a proper diet). We recommend starting with one drop of the desired oil mixed in their food. Some cats also like NingXia Red and a drop of oil may be added to that liquid (keeping in mind there are already certain oils in the NingXia Red).

Birds

As a general rule, using a cold air or nebulizing diffuser is usually the preferred method of administering essential oils to our companion birds for several reasons. Birds have air sacs (similar to lungs) all over their bodies and a diffuser will distribute the essential oils into the air sacs so as to be absorbed throughout the bird's body very effectively. A diffuser placed near the cage or perch where the bird is works very effectively most of the time. All of the guidelines for diffusing previously stated apply to birds as well: make sure fresh air is always available and do not diffuse for extended periods of time.

It has been found that birds thrive, with the addition of therapeutic grade essential oils in their lives.

Topical application may be desired in some situations, e.g. in cases of organ diseases, tumors, broken bones etc; the essential oil(s) should be diluted with a carrier oil. Applying diluted essential oils to the feathers will matt the feathers, so please do not do this. If topical application is needed applying to the bottom of the feet is the recommended method as the feet can handle the carrier oils; the essential oils will still enter the bloodstream via the feet. An indirect method of administering oils to a bird's feet is to place a drop or two of oil on your palm, rub palms together and then rub the perch in the bird's cage. Spritzing is another way to topically administer oils to birds. Mix a few drops of essential oil in a spray bottle with distilled water and a drop of Animal Scents shampoo to emulsify, shake well and mist the bird.

Orally, essential oils can be added to the bird's drinking water at a rate of one drop per liter of clean water.

Delivery Methods

There are three basic ways to use or apply essential oils to the animal:

Olfactory:
    Diffusion
    Inhalation

Topically:
    Water Misting & Soaking
    Raindrop Technique
    Petting Technique
    Ting Point Therapy (horses)

Internal Consumption

Please see the sections at the end of "Safe Use" regarding cats and birds.

Olfactory

Diffusion

Diffusion of essential oils into the air of an enclosed space (such as a house, kennel or aviary) is popularly called aromatherapy. The aromatic molecules of the essential oils are literally breathed into the body, at which point they trigger numerous immune boosting, healing, relaxation or stimulation responses depending upon the specific oils being inhaled.

When an essential oil is diffused (or otherwise inhaled), it is processed through the olfactory system, which then sends the therapeutic benefits of the aroma to the brain. Depending on the specific constituents in the particular oil being diffused, the body may begin to feel the release of negative emotions, the soothing of undue muscle tension, or experience a "cleansing" effect. Young Living Founder, D. Gary Young points out that the body's response time to inhalation of essential oils can be as quick as one to three seconds!

This is why with many people and household pets, inhalation of diffused oils is the preferred method of using essential oils. Essential oils when diffused may clear the air of many allergens, toxins, and noxious odors; they may help relieve symptoms ranging from sneezing and allergies to listlessness and depression. The higher frequency of the essential oil constituents, when diffused, can also help to clear the air of pathogenic microbes. Diffusing essential oils into a room with a sick pet (or human family member) with respiratory issues may actually cut their downtime by half or more; and regular diffusion of essential oils throughout the year may help to keep these conditions in check. According to Dr. Valnet: "Many essences (e.g. cinnamon, pine [needles], thyme, lemon) have marked effects on this condition [influenza], and patients [human] that have been treated with these essences for a variety of complaints seem to get through the winter without trouble." (Valnet and Tisserand 1982, p66) [text added]

Diffusing essential oils for horses in a stable is more difficult because the space is typically not (or should not be) enclosed (nor should the horse be kept in an enclosed space except for temporary therapeutic purposes). But even more importantly, it actually may be contraindicated. Neg-ions attach themselves to particles of dust, pollution, and moisture, losing their charge. This can actually cause an "overdose" of pos-ions. And horse stables are, by nature, rather dusty, humid places. The preferred olfactory method for horses is offering direct inhalation. If one is in a hospital setting for some reason that would then be a more ideal situation to diffuse essential oils for horses.

Types of Diffusers

The most popular and effective method of diffusing oils is a type of diffuser called a cold air, nebulizing, or atomizing diffuser. It does not use water and sprays an ultra-fine mist of only the essential oil into the air. The millions of misted particles sprayed from a diffuser are so fine they can hang in the air literally for hours, spreading from room to room via the normal air circulation. These are typically the most expensive type of diffuser, but the one from which you will receive the maximum benefit. Atomizing type diffusers have another benefit inasmuch as the high velocity with which the oil is dispersed energizes and increases the frequency of the oil. (Stewart 2004, p444)

Diffusers that use water (distilled) are another type. However, since essential oils are hydrophobic (adverse to water), they will generally float on top of the water while some oils are denser than water and will not float. These fan-powered evaporative type diffusers will blow out the lightest molecules first before the heavier ones. In other words, you never get the whole oil into the air at the same time. (Stewart 2004, p443)

Atomizing Diffuser

Essential oils can be diffused into the air in a couple of ways if you don't have a diffuser. While not as effective as actually diffusing them, during summer months when you have a fan or air conditioner running, one of the simplest ways to diffuse is to put a few drops of your favorite oil onto a tissue and secure the tissue next to the air vent or the fan cage so that the air blows across it. The blowing air then circulates the aromatic molecules of the essential oil throughout the space, and your pets (and you) breathe them in as you go about your normal daily activities.

You can also use a little 4 – 6 oz "mister" or spray bottle and fill it with distilled or spring water, add 15 or 20 drops of essential oil, shake well, and then walk through your home and/or kennel briefly "misting" each room or area with the solution as you go. Again, remember that essential oils and water do not truly mix, so you will not be misting all the molecules of the oil (although it still smells good!); you can always add just a drop of some kind of liquid soap to help emulsify and disperse the spray better.

> NOTE: Always use cold or room temperature diffusion. NEVER HEAT ESSENTIAL OILS, as in boiling them in water to diffuse, for instance. Heat distillation can alter the chemistry, rendering them therapeutically useless. That being said, if you should forget and leave a closed bottle of a "true" (i.e. distilled) essential oil in the car on a hot day do not panic and throw it away. Just do not open the bottle until it cools back down. The expressed oils (includes all the citrus oils) and the absolutes (e.g. Neroli, Jasmine, and Onycha) and any blends that contain these, however, do need to be kept at temperatures less than 100ºF and 90ºF or 38ºC and 28ºC, respectively. (Stewart 2004, pp431-435)

<u>Inhalation</u>

Inhalation of essential oils is also a very effective manner of dosing. It is the preferred olfactory method for horses for the reasons stated above. As we briefly discussed before, animals have an extremely keen sense of smell and tend to have a more correct way of inhaling – in fact they tend to breathe generally more correctly than we humans do! Never force an animal to inhale a particular oil, always allow them the opportunity to turn away. Sometimes they will turn away and then come back for another sniff. Be patient and give her time to work through the process. Keeping the head turned away or walking away is a sure sign the animal is either done with the oil or does not like it in the first place. You can pick two or three oils to try; give the animal several minutes in between each offering to allow them to "clear the head". Never place the bottle directly under the nose, always hold it about two or three inches away. If there is a keen interest, you can also place a drop or two on your hand and allow the animal a chance to lick the oil. Please note, if they do lick in this manner, this is called a "neat" application (i.e. not diluted) and would be contraindicated for hot oils (e.g. clove, cinnamon, oregano, etc). That being said, there are some animals that ingesting hot oils does not seem to bother.

Either way (diffusion or direct inhalation) of breathing in essential oils is extremely effective due to their small molecular size and volatility. All of their molecules can easily pass into the olfactory system directly into the blood stream via the lungs, or they can pass directly into the central brain. (Stewart 2004, p111)

These are some suggestions for oils to use:
- Anxiety or stress
  singles: Lavender, Roman chamomile, Vetiver
  blends: Harmony, Joy, Peace & Calming, RutaVaLa, Stress Away

- Immune support
  singles: Frankincense, Melissa, Peppermint, Rose
  blends: ImmuPower, Thieves

- Respiratory support
  singles: Cedarwood, Cypress, Dorado Azul, Lauris noblis, Lemon myrtle, Myrtle
  blends: R.C., Raven

This is just a small list of suggestions; different essential oils can be diffused or inhaled for different effects. For example, Frankincense and Lavender can also soothe and calm. The blend, Acceptance, can help ease the situation of introducing a new puppy into the household. Joy, along with Peace & Calming, or Lavender are often used for their calming and emotionally balancing effects. Purification, Lemon or Thieves blend can purify the air and neutralize mildew, cigarette smoke, synthetic fragrances and negate the effects of pathogens as well as repel pests.

Topically

When applied topically, essential oils penetrate directly into the body via the small blood capillaries in the skin. There are several factors that can affect the rate of absorption. A carrier oil will slow down the rate of absorption. The area of skin size makes a difference; in other words, when applying diluted essential oils topically, the smaller the area of application, the less EO is absorbed. Comparing undiluted essential oils to water, the oils being highly lipophilic they can absorb through the skin much faster than water does (some say 100 times faster). Essential oils applied to areas of subcutaneous fat (which contain less blood capillaries) and mature or dehydrated skin will also cause the rate of absorption to slow down. (Fioravanti 2011, p68), (Verspoor and Decker 2000, p396) If there are any concerns about using oils neat for any animal, always dilute with organic olive oil, Young Living's V6 oil, or similar. Applying a carrier oil after application of a neat essential oil will remove undesirable effects – such as a burning sensation when using the hotter oils. Applying a thin layer of carrier oil prior to the application of any essential oil can place a barrier on the skin that can slow down the rate of absorption. Just remember – never attempt to counteract an essential oil with water; you will only intensify the effects that you want to remove.

A note about "diluting" with a carrier oil: As stated above, mixing essential oils with a carrier oil will slow down the rate of absorption. It is important to understand that this is not truly diluting the effectiveness of the essential oil, it just takes longer for the therapeutic benefits to be realized by the body. This is all within reason of course; if the British school of dilution is followed (diluting by about 90%-95%), you will then certainly lose effectiveness and potential for healing. (Stewart 2004, p479) All Young Living essential oils state whether they are safe to use topically and whether they should be diluted or not. The rate of dilution for animals depends upon the species as well as the intent for applying the oil.

When applying oils to the skin, also keep in mind that each individual may react a bit differently to the oils as each individual has a different body chemistry; proteins can affect the way an essential oil "behaves" when applied topically. Sweat of course contains proteins; dogs and cats sweat through their pads while horses (and humans) sweat through their skin.

> Please Note: Oils containing furanoid compounds can be phototoxic and may cause sunburn; do NOT apply these oils and allow the animal to go into sunshine for several hours afterward (these oils are best applied at night); applies to topical use only, not internal consumption. The phototoxic oils include: Angelica, Anise, Bergamot, Bitter Orange (Neroli: only ones that are expressed, not absolutes), Cumin, Fennel, Grapefruit, Lemon, Lime, Petitgrain, Rue; as well as any of the blends containing these singles. This applies whether diluted or not. (Stewart 2004, pp381-382) Also check the Desk Reference if in doubt.

> Do not use Fennel, Hyssop, or wild Tansy in animals that are suspected of being seizure-prone or having high blood pressure.

<u>Water Misting & Soaking</u>

Water misting is appropriate especially for birds (please see section on Safe Use) and may also work great for other animals. Misting can also be used for applying your own oil blends for flies, fleas or ticks to your animals. Simply put several drops of the oil or oils you want to use into a dark (brown or blue) glass bottle and add spring or distilled water to bring near the top. Then add one or two drops (depending on the size of the bottle, you don't need much) of Animal Scents shampoo or Thieves household cleaner to emulsify/blend the oils; shake well before misting. For small animals, a four or six ounce bottle is generally sufficient to keep from having to refill often. For larger animals, such as horses, you will of course want a larger bottle. Since glass is generally a "no-no" in and around barns, thick plastic spray bottles can be used. Some essential oils can dissolve plastic and it is not recommended to store them undiluted in plastic. However, in practice, putting 20-30 drops each of various oils (typically about five or six different singles) into a 16 oz. spray bottle with two or three drops of Animal Scents shampoo and distilled water to fill has not presented a problem. Putting at least some water in first before any of the oils is highly recommended. And of course, shake well before each use.

Soaking is another method of essential oil application with animals. Fill basin or tub with warm water and a few drops of Animal Scents shampoo or Thieves household cleaner and several drops of the oil or oils of your choice; swish the oils through the water and put their feet or hooves in the water or for smaller animals, place the entire body into the water depending on what you want soaked. The oils in the water will be absorbed through the skin.

Raindrop Technique

The Raindrop technique (generally referred to as "RDT") was initially created by Gary Young in the 1980's for humans; it has since been adapted for various animal species by different individuals. While in general essential oils work as much if not more through the "unseen" energetic realm as the physical, RDT especially is much more about changing the frequency of the organism than it is about the various oils' immediate chemical effects toward microbes. It can be a very powerful healing tool, working more within the etheric (life force) realm than

Shadrach ready for his Raindrop session

directly in the physical realm – which of course we will then see the benefits manifest in the physical realm. The technique is basically to drop the oils along the spine (like gentle raindrops), holding the bottle approximately six inches above the body. In using RDT we address (some of) the chakras, which are the astral energy centers that have corresponding plexuses in the physical body. Dropping the oils a short distance from the body allows them to flow through the body's electromagnetic (EM) field; in this way we are making an energetic "connection" between the three bodies (astral, etheric, and physical) and enhancing the flow of the cerebral spinal fluid. Some of the physical benefits you may see with RDT are pain relief from joint/bone challenges and possibly even improve the condition; relaxing and calming for anxiety issues; pest deterrent; immune boosting and gentle detoxing.

This technique can be done either "neat" – meaning not diluted with a fatty oil, or they can be applied diluted; it all depends upon the oils you use and the species of animal you are working with. We do not recommend applying any essential oil, even those from Young Living, in a neat form to cats or birds in a Raindrop session.[19] (Please see the section on Safe Use for more discussion.) And again, the only essential oils we recommend to apply topically in a neat manner (or any manner) are those from Young Living. How much you dilute the essential oil(s) will depend upon the animal as well as the intended purpose of application.

Understanding just a little bit about how the oils work from within their own chemistry in layering during RDT can help you to understand how and when to use this powerful technique as well as knowing how to substitute oils when needed or even desired. There is a fairly simple acronym, based upon three of the major chemical compounds found in essential oils, that Dr. David Stewart uses to assess the order in which the oils should be applied (if this is the intent to begin with). He calls it "PMS" (which should be easy enough for us women to remember!), although in actual practice is should read "PSM". Also, this theory applies just as much to inhalation and oral applications as it does to RDT and other topical methods. The theory is basically this: (Stewart 2004, 291-293)

Phenols – those oils high in phenols are used first as they have the capability to clean the cellular receptor sites

Sesquiterpenes – oils high in sesquiterpenes are used next in layering as the can delete bad information from cellular memory

Monoterpenes – the oils high in this compound are lastly used to restore and awaken the correct information in the DNA (cellular memory)

The *Essential Oils Desk Reference* generally gives the percentages of these compounds in the oils listed. Beginning on page 502 of *The Chemistry of Essential Oils Made Simple*, you can find a listing of the chemical analyses in most essential oils: pg 571, Table Forty-Eight is the percent of Phenol content; pg 572, Table Forty-Nine is the Sesquiterpene table; and pg 569, Table Forty-Six is the Monoterpene content. (See Recommended Resources section for both of these books.)

Another way to utilize a variation of RDT is by selecting six or seven single oils based upon their frequency from lower to higher. These can be applied in one session or over a period of time. The healthier the animal, the more "charge" the organism can take; those animals that are not in a healthy state to begin with may not be able to handle high frequency levels straight away. We invite you to consider that those animals with chronic, debilitating conditions would benefit from a RDT session of this nature spread out over a week's period. In other words, beginning with the lowest frequency of the chosen oils on the first day and following in increasing frequency each day for six or seven days depending upon the number of oils chosen. This would allow the animal to adjust to the frequency level before asking the organism to "tune up" another octave.

---

[19] Also please do not shave the animal prior to applying RDT, regardless of what oils you use, but especially if using hot oils.

(And yes, frequencies in essential oils can be thought of as musical notes to assist the body in "tuning up".)

Resources to help you learn RDT for animals include the Young Living *Essential Oils Desk Reference, 5th Ed* and DVD's published by Veterinarian Dr. Nancy Brandt on using raindrop technique, one for dogs and one for horses, as well as the RDT kit directly from Young Living (for human but instructional nevertheless). They can be purchased from the Abundant Health website Books & Media shop:

http://www.abundanthealth4u.com/DVD_Raindrop_Technique_for_Dogs_p/8604dvd.htm
http://www.abundanthealth4u.com/DVD_Raindrop_Technique_for_Horses_p/8603dvd.htm
http://www.youngliving.com/en_US/products/essential-oils/massage-oils/raindrop-technique-essential-oil-collection

Above all, just remember there can be variations on anyone's method. Try it and allow it to grow with you and your animal, and as always be open and receptive to what the animal is telling you.

Petting Technique

As with RDT, this technique can be done using the oils either neat or diluted. This technique is well tolerated by most animals and in fact may be the easiest topical method to use with cats. For smaller animals, drip a couple of drops of the essential oil you want to use into the palm of one hand. With your other palm, put your hands together and swirl the oils a few times to activate them and spread them to both palms. Then simply pet the animal, fluffing the coat. For large animal such as horses, you will likely have to repeat this technique two or three times to cover the entire body; otherwise, just a particular area (shoulder for example) may be all that needs to receive the petting. As a variant of this, with horses especially, you can rub the oil between your hands and "hold" the area (with proper intent), letting the horse guide you in how long and where.

<u>Ting Point Therapy for Horses</u>

Ting point therapy is based upon classic meridian concepts of Traditional Chinese Medicine (TCM).[20] Ting points are the beginning or ending of an associated meridian and are located on the coronary band of the front and hind legs; the six points are positioned roughly equal distance around the circumference of the coronary band. The importance is to view them in relation to each other; those that are not balanced can look and feel different from the others. These TCM points can provide valuable information about the general health of the horse, and with practice, one can detect meridian imbalances and disease conditions. (Zidonis *et al.* 2001, pp72-73) Essential oils can be used very effectively on these ting points in the same general way that acupressure is applied. Place two or three drops of the desired essential oil (single or blend) in a palm and use a finger of the opposite hand, dipped in the oil, to apply appropriate pressure to the ting point – either chosen point(s) for specific issues or all of them for balancing. Equine ting point charts are available in the book, *Equine Acupressure, A Working Manual* available from Tallgrass Publishers (see Recommended Resources section).

Please note that it is not just horses that have these ting points; any being that has a life force has energy meridians. And in fact, essential oils can be used in conjunction with any acupressure therapy, whole body or localized, although some practitioners can balance the whole animal using the ting points alone. If you are familiar with acupressure, this may be a good way to incorporate essential oils into your animal's life; the oils may be used in one or all phases of the acupressure session depending upon need and intent.

Internal Consumption

Among the ways to use essential oils, the least understood seems to be internal use. Yet, when used properly internal use offers potent therapeutic benefits. As with any delivery method, internal use of essential oils can support the organ systems, and balance the metabolism. Obviously internal dosing of essential oils means they must go through the digestive system. Essential oils can be destroyed to a certain extent by acids in the stomach (Stewart 2004, p350), up to 80% in humans; the best time (for humans) to ingest essential oils is on an empty stomach such as first thing in the morning[21]. While there is no hard data to our knowledge on other species regarding best time to give an oil, a basic understanding of animal physiology and biological dietary requirements can give us a clue. The destruction by stomach acid does not mean the oils are rendered useless, quite the contrary. The molecules of a therapeutic grade essential oil will engulf and

---

[20] Saunders Comprehensive Veterinary Dictionary 3rd Edition. D.C. Blood, V.P. Studdert and C.C. Gay, Elsevier, 2007. Answers.com 18 May. 2014. http://www.answers.com/topic/ting-point-therapy

[21] From an article by David Stewart, <u>When is the Best Time to Take Oils Internally</u>; http://www.raindroptraining.com/messenger/v5n1.html#internally

neutralize the free hydrogen ions that have potential to cause physiological harm when in circulation. (Stewart 2004, p350) We can also exit the material realm of chemistry long enough to understand that, even if the oils are not intact physically (i.e. measurably) after digestion as they were when ingested, their healing messages are still very much alive.

In practice, what this means for the carnivores in our life (cats and dogs) is that administering the oils internally should also occur as close as possible on an empty stomach. For dogs fed a species appropriate diet this is not generally an issue as they are not (should not be) fed continuously. Cats can present a bit of a different issue inasmuch as they require more frequent feedings. And as well, most cats may be adverse to the taste of essential oils. After all, they naturally only partake of anything from the plant world when they need an emetic. Horses may seemingly present an issue with regard to administering oils on an empty stomach as they are "trickle feeders" requiring content in their stomachs almost on a frequent basis (and therefore a frequent influx of stomach acid). There are times when horses (at least those that are allowed natural lives) are idle and not eating much, which would be the best times to administer essential oils internally if possible.

All this being said, these are guidelines and not to cause undue concern in those who may be starting out using essential oils. As you begin to get more familiar with their use with your animal, you will know intuitively when to use which method of application. And again, we suggest that the healing power of essential oils lies not wholly within their physicality or their measurable chemical components.

Many Young Living Essential oils are certified as GRAS (Generally Regarded as Safe) by the FDA. If an essential oil does not have GRAS certification on the label, it will NOT be safe to use internally. Please remember that oils that are safe to use with humans internally are not always safe to use with animals internally, especially with cats, birds and other small animals. We only use and recommend Young Living essential oils due to the company's integrity and extensive knowledge of the entire process from organic growing through processing to seal.

To administer essential oils to dogs and horses you may put two or three drops into empty gelatin capsules, place in or on a small bit of food or species appropriate treat; they may also be dripped into the mouth if the animal is willing for this. Some dogs and horses don't mind the taste of the oils and will lick them from the palm of your hand. The important thing to remember here is to know your animal. You should know what their tolerances, likes and dislikes are, and again, please allow the animal to guide you in this. (Please see section on Safe Use concerning using essential oils with cats and birds.)

Putting the Oils into Action

Using these volatile wonders of nature forms an integral part of holistic living and healing. There are many ways in which essential oils can be used in daily living, from dealing with tangible aspects (fleas, skin infections, etc) to the intangible (e.g. emotional issues). Not only do they smell wonderful, when diffused they can clean the air naturally while negating the harmful effects of bacteria and viruses.

Following each of the sub-sections below will be some suggestions on which oils to choose; check the EODR (*Essential Oils Desk Reference*) or other reference source for more information (see Recommended Resources section). Some of these oils are already blends, but any of the singles can be used alone or combined with a few other synergistic singles to make your own blend. As we've mentioned several times, always try to involve your animal in the decision-making process of which oil(s) to use. Also remember that there is not just "one correct oil" to use in a given situation. The oils act and react with the organism's own chemistry to create something unique, so keep in mind that the listed actions of an essential oil will not always happen in every individual animal.

Balancing the Emotions

Emotions have links to health and well-being for both animals and humans. Stress and emotional trauma can weaken the immune system and delay healing. Today, we live in a society of emotional turmoil. If an animal has been adopted from a shelter or rescue situation, almost always there has been emotional trauma in this animal's life. There is more focus on emotional behavior and psychological conditions in all animals, including humans, now than at any time in our history. And we are beginning to realize that the physical healing process cannot truly complete without healing the higher bodies – the life force and the soul where our animals are concerned. Many animal health practitioners are recognizing the aspect that a number of physical conditions are caused by emotional problems that link back to your animal's "babyhood". We are also realizing just how much our own emotions – good or bad – affect our animals.

Throughout history, essential oils have been used for not just physical healing but for emotional and spiritual healing as well. Chemically we now know that smelling activates the limbic system, affecting the amygdala gland where memories are stored. Through the limbic system we gain access to the other bodies, including the astral (soul) body which is the seat of emotions. Inhaling the essential oils evokes a "release" of stored emotions from cellular memory, thus clearing the astral and etheric bodies and facilitating healing at the physical level. Essential oils can play an important role in assisting the animals (and us humans) to move beyond these emotional barriers. The aldehydes and esters of certain essential oils are very calming and sedating to the central nervous system, including both the sympathetic and para-sympathetic systems. These substances allow the animal to relax instead of letting anxiety build up in the body. We know from research of scientists such as Bruce Lipton that emotions can affect gene expression. (Lipton 2008, p37) When certain detrimental emotions (such as anxiety) are sustained for or repeated over a length of time, the genetic expression can convert into abnormal somatic conditions (aka, "physical diseases").

Domestic animals are subject to many things foreign to their nature, not the least of which are vaccines – that contain multiple toxins – and processed diets which are completely inappropriate for their physiology. We have already mentioned that species appropriate diet underlies all health; and while we won't go into detail about the vaccines, suffice it to say the authors of this book are actively against conventional vaccination (but do support the use of nosodes/homeopathic vaccines which are completely safe and effective). While we sincerely hope that you would not use toxic vaccines and that you would feed a species-appropriate diet, many of us take on animals that have had at least exposure to incorrect diets and vaccines in their previous home. When an animal is exposed to the toxins in vaccines and the animal equivalent of "junk" food, their physical body not only may react directly but this can also cause changes in the other bodies as well, including the astral; and the astral body being the seat of emotions this can in turn generate reactive type emotions, sometimes manifesting as "obsessive" behavior. The reactive emotions, if sustained unduly, can trigger somatic issues, and you then find yourself on a merry-go-round. Also keep in mind that many times emotions that our animals manifest are reflections of our own emotions. So when we do an oil session with the animal, we can be just as affected by emotional releases if not more so than the animal is.

Some method of inhalation (diffusing or direct from the bottle) and/or topically (e.g. petting or raindrop) are generally the best ways to administer essential oils for emotional work.

- For anger/aggression or agitation
  singles: Bergamot, Cedarwood, Clary Sage, Frankincense, Geranium, Juniper, Lavender, Marjoram, Myrrh, Roman Chamomile, Rose, Ylang Ylang, Sandalwood
  blends: Chivalry, Forgiveness, Harmony, Joy, Peace & Calming, Release, Sacred Mountain, Surrender, Valor

- For past abuse
  singles: Geranium, Melissa, Sandalwood
  blends: Forgiveness, Grounding, Hope, Inner Child, Joy, Peace & Calming, SARA, Trauma Life, Valor, White Angelica

- For concentration/clarification
  singles: Frankincense, Galbanum, Melissa, Sandalwood

- For emotional clearing/release
  blends: Release, Trauma Life

- For fear/phobias
  <u>singles</u>: Bergamot, Clary Sage, Cypress, Geranium, Idaho Blue Spruce, Juniper, Lavender, Marjoram, Myrrh, Orange, Patchouli, Roman Chamomile, Sandalwood, Spruce, Rose, Ylang Ylang

- For obsessive behavior
  <u>singles</u>: Clary Sage, Cypress, Geranium, Helichrysum, Lavender, Marjoram, Rose, Sandalwood, Ylang Ylang
  <u>blends</u>: Acceptance, Awaken, Forgiveness, Humility, Inner Child, Motivation, Present Time, Sacred Mountain, Surrender, Valor

Detoxification

An often times misunderstood function of the body is detoxification. Detoxification is a normal metabolic process. When the animal's diet and lifestyle follows the laws of nature appropriate for the species, detoxification will naturally occur and most of the time we barely notice this process. Occasionally the animal may display short-lived symptoms (depending on the species) such as itching, sneezing, runny noses, runny and/or goopy eyes, loose stools, vomiting, lethargy, etc. This can be a normally heightened immune response to either particular emotional events and/or environmental stressors, such as increased pollen count, etc. It is not necessarily cause for alarm (i.e. thinking the animal is getting "sick") and a healthy animal will generally resolve the issues quickly. Using essential oils to support a healthy animal will keep these kinds of immune reactions to a minimum; a regular Raindrop technique is a very beneficial way to help keep the animal's emunctory system flowing properly. In more serious situations (please see note below), the oils can assist in easing some of the attenuating healing reactions.

> If the animal is already ill and/or has a history of processed diet and vaccinations, etc, once you begin to resolve these issues, the animal may indeed begin to express the symptomology of major detoxification symptoms (aka "healing reactions") and this can quickly become complicated. It is in these kinds of situations that, unless you are experienced in this, we strongly recommend you consult with a qualified animal health coach that can help you through the process. Most veterinarians are not trained to think in this manner and view each symptom as a "disease" and want to prescribe suppressive drugs.

Some suggested essential oils:

Angelica (Angelica archangelica) invigorates the lymph system; also acts on water retention and is believed to have beneficial effects on the liver. Angelica blends especially well with citrus essential oils. Angelica is a phototoxic oil (see Note in Materia Medica section).

Cedarwood (Cedrus atlantica) oil contains the highest known concentration of sesquiterpenes – up to 98%, (Stewart ©2002, p135) and is believed to have high capability of being able to repair damaged DNA. This DNA 're-set' capability is further believed to be enhanced when used in conjunction with Frankincense oil.

Coriander (Coriandrum sativum) oil is known for its digestive, analgesic, and sedative properties; it may also help facilitate the removal of heavy metals and act as a hepatoprotective. (Aga *et al.* 2001), (Samojlik *et al.* 2010)

Frankincense (Boswellia carteri) oil contains high levels of monoterpenes – up to 90% (Stewart 2004, p513); monoterpenes are believed to have the capability to reprogram cellular memory and maintain cellular regeneration (Stewart ©2002, p292); it has been well studied for it effects in cancer remediation.[22] Use in combination with Cedarwood for enhanced effect on DNA.

Geranium (Pelargonium) is one of the best essential oils for the skin; it also stimulates the liver and kidneys, and helps the immune system, promoting blood circulation. Its soothing aroma makes it perfect to blend with angelica, grapefruit or orange.

Grapefruit (Citrus paradise) oil has a diuretic effect, and can aid the digestive system and skin. It refreshes the mind, relieves anxiety, is reviving, uplifting, and helps disperse negative energy. This is a phototoxic oil.

Helichrysum (Helichrysum italicum) oil is ideal for use in the more serious situations such as a vaccine/drug detox (see note above). It helps stimulate liver cells, thin mucous secretions, and acts as a free radical scavenger. It is non-irritating.

Juniper (Juniperus communis) oil is a powerful purifier, helping to avert nervous tension; it is recognized to reduce cellulite in humans. Juniper can help expel uric acid from the system. Its spicy aroma helps to strengthen and fortify the spirit during times of low energy, anxiety, and emotional overload.

---

[22] Searching in Google Scholar for "HK Lin frankincense" (without quotes) will bring up several cancer studies on Frankincense.

<u>Laurel (Laurus nobilis)</u> oil is characterized by a fresh, sweet smell; it contains eugenol which makes it effective in thinning mucous secretions, as an expectorant, and in deactivating viral and fungal microbial forms. According to chemist Kurt Schnaubelt, laurel has a supportive effect on the lymphatic system; he suggests rubbing a few drops directly on swollen lymph nodes for an immediate effect. (Schnaubelt 1999, p228)

<u>Ledum (Ledum groenlandicum)</u> may be helpful for liver and kidney support and may help resolve diseases of the kidneys and liver. It may also be helpful in reducing tumors.

<u>Lemon (Citrus limonum)</u> is a refreshing citrus oil; it helps stimulate white blood cells; it helps support and cleanse the liver. Lemon oil can aid in bringing clarity to the mind and emotions. Lemon is a phototoxic.

<u>Roman chamomile (Chamaemelum nobile)</u> is another oil that can cleanse the liver and blood. It can also help to release anger and balance the emotions.

Insects and Internal Parasites

Many commercial insecticides and insect repellents contain poisonous ingredients that are toxic to animals, humans and the environment. Young Living therapeutic grade essential oils are safe, effective alternatives to noxious, synthetic formulas. Young Living also has some essential oil infused supplements that can be used as safe "de-worming" agents. Unless there is some other mitigating factor(s), animals that are cared for species-appropriately (with regard to diet and lifestyle) are not going to suffer ill effects from internal parasites. While in-depth discussion of internal parasites is outside the intent of this book, understanding that an animal having some amount of parasites is a completely normal occurrence is tantamount to keeping them healthy. We suggest either having fecal counts done at the appropriate time and/or becoming comfortable with the external signs of a high level infestation so you will know when to act. Also remember that a high level internal parasite infestation is not the cause but is the result of another underlying etiology. In other words, the "bugs" proliferated due to some kind of imbalance. We sincerely hope you do not use chemical de-wormers as they have been found to cause auto-immune deficiencies and diseases in animals.

The essential oils can be used to make into a spray that can be used topically on the animal or on and within the animal's environment. As practitioners, we have found therapeutic essential oils to be some of the most effective, safe and reliable insect deterrents you can find.

- Fleas, Mosquitoes, Ticks
  <u>singles</u>: Cedarwood, Eucalyptus radiata, Geranium, Idaho Tansy, Lavender, Lemongrass, Myrrh, Ocotea, Palo Santo, Peppermint, Rosewood, Spearmint, Thyme

blends: Purification

- Ants, Aphids, Chiggers
  singles: Cedarwood, Hyssop, Lavender, Lemongrass, Peppermint, Sage, Spearmint, Thyme

- Flies, Gnats, Lice
  singles: Cedarwood, Lavender, Patchouli, Peppermint, Rosemary, Sage, Spearmint

- Internal parasites
  blends: DiGize
  supplements: ParaFree

Joint and Muscle Pain

Topical application of essential oils is a wonderful opportunity to combine them with some kind of massage therapy, including T-Touch, Bowen Therapy, etc.

- singles: Balsam fir, Copaiba (warming), Juniper, Peppermint (cooling)
- blends: Deep Relief, En-R-Gee, Panaway, R.C., Relieve It
- supplements: BLM (note: capsules only for dogs/cats; powder contains xylitol but is ok for use in horses)[23], Sulfurzyme

Pathogens

Microbes in the form of bacteria, viruses, and fungi exist everywhere. Professor Antoine Béchamp, who lived at the same time as Louis Pasteur, developed and demonstrated the pleomorphic theory that bacteria change form (in both shape and size), having the capability to evolve and devolve depending upon the internal terrain of the body. These concepts were subsequently verified by the research work of people such as Royal Raymond Rife, Gaston Naessens, Gunter Enderlein, Wilhelm Reich, and Dr. Sam Chachoua. Under the principles of pleomorphism[24], there is no such concept as "good" or "bad" bacteria (etc) – the bacteria (or virus, yeast, fungi) are simply a state of

---

[23] Xylitol can cause an insulin dump which appears to be species specific. This is known to occur in dogs and is almost immediate leading to a rapid drop in blood sugar. It is not known whether it occurs in cats or not but to be on the safe side we recommend do not give as they are also carnivores. Horses do not seem to be affected by xylitol regarding insulin release; we nevertheless recommend that you use caution and observe the horse while on BLM powder form.

See this: http://healthypets.mercola.com/sites/healthypets/archive/2011/03/24/dangers-of-xylitol-for-pet-dogs.aspx

[24] For further information, the American Council of Animal Naturopathy has an online course on pleomorphism.

being in response to the terrain. These microbes are not the causal factor, but are the resulting factor of so-called disease, many times being the result of incorrect nutrition. Microbes morph into a pathogenic state because there is a disturbance in the body. Unfortunately, Béchamp was more interested in valid science than in the accolades that Pasteur was after; and so Pasteur's monomorphic "germ theory" was passed down, becoming the central dogma of current microbiological science, which remains in a stronghold position to this day.

Antibiotics never "cure"; they suppress the condition and depress the immune system by decreasing the number of circulating white blood cells and the body always reacts again, sooner or later, after a round of antibiotics, even if not in the same way. This in turn lowers the animal's ability to fight "infections". Antibiotics disrupt the normal population of microbes existing in a symbiotic state in the gastrointestinal tract of all animals; terrain-specific microbial colonies are the first line of defense against most "diseases", and without them the animal is more susceptible. Some antibiotics, such as chloramphenicol, can cause irreversible damage to the bone marrow. We are seeing a proliferation of bacteria morphing to a stage in which they are resistant to the effects of antibiotics.

When we use essentials oils for pathogens, our purpose is to help bring the body back into harmony or equilibrium, creating an internal state in which the microbes return – or devolve – to their non-pathogenic form, and are no longer "seen" under typical microscope. It is this effect that is deemed via conventional science to be "anti"-pathogenic. And it is this communicative effect on the pleomorphic stages that ensures that essential oils can never become "resistant" to various stages of microbes, as opposed to conventional anti-microbial substances which work only in an antagonistic, suppressive manner.

Essential oils can be used for pathogenic situations via any of the delivery methods previously described. Some of the oils – such as the Eucalyptus singles and blends containing it – are excellent for diffusing to help breathing issues that are common in respiratory situations. Almost all therapeutic essential oils have some effect on microbes; below are some of the more common ones that research has indicated most effective in particular microbial states.

- Bacteria
  singles: Cinnamon, Clove, Lemon, Melaleuca, Mountain Savory, Oregano, Ravintsara, Thyme, Eucalyptus (all species…E.citriodora, E.dives, E.globulus & E.radiata)
  blends: Exodus II, ImmuPower, Inspiration, Melrose, Sacred Mountain, Thieves
  supplements: ImmuPro, InnerDefense, Super C.

- Viruses
  singles: Basil, Cinnamon Bark, Clove, Eucalyptus (all species), Galbanum, Hyssop, Jasmine, Marjoram, Melaleuca, Melissa, Mountain Savory, Myrrh, Oregano
  blends: Exodus II, ImmuPower, Thieves

<u>supplements</u>: Inner Defense

Skin Issues and Wounds

For skin issues, topical application (including Raindrop) of essential oils is the preferred method in conjunction with internal delivery as needed. Internal method (can dilute and place in a capsule) is preferred for the "hot" oils such as Oregano, especially being undesirable on sensitive, damaged skin.

- Mange mites
 <u>singles</u>: Anise, Lavender, Lemongrass, Melaleuca
 <u>blends</u>: Purification

- Yeast
 <u>singles</u>: Laurus nobilis, Myrrh, Oregano[25]

- Hot spots
 <u>singles</u>: Helichrysum, Lavender, Myrrh, Patchouli
 <u>blends</u>: Animal Scents Ointment

- Wounds
 <u>singles</u>: Lavender, Melrose, Roman chamomile
 <u>blends</u>: Animal Scents Ointment

- Bleeding, bruising, pain
 <u>singles</u>: Cistus (particularly effective with hematomas), Helichrysum, Idaho Tansy, Roman Chamomile, Tsuga
 <u>supplements</u>: Sulfurzyme

- Tissue regeneration
 <u>singles</u>: Geranium, Helichrysum, Idaho balsam fir, Patchouli
 blends: Thieves

---

[25] There has been a recent (April 2014) study on the successful resolution of canine Malassezia Dermatitis using essential oils; see here: http://healthimpactnews.com/2014/study-essential-oils-and-coconut-oil-effective-for-skin-disorders-on-dogs/

Ylang Ylang flower

Ylang Ylang(Cananga odorata) – pronounced "EE-lăng-EE-lăng" – is a tropical evergreen tree originating in the Philippines. It grows quickly in its native climate, about 15 feet per year, eventually reaching 80 feet. The essential oil is distilled from the flowers, which only appear on the standard tree at maturity… about five years of age. Much of the current world's supply of Ylang Ylang essential oil is produced in Madagascar and the Comoro Islands in the Indian Ocean. Young Living Ylang Ylang is grown on the company's farm located in Guayaquil, Ecuador, consisting of about 2000 acres; peppermint, lemongrass, and Palo Santo trees are also grown there. Ylang Ylang flowers must be harvested at just the right time of day as well as the correct rate of maturity in order to produce a high quality oil. The essential oils are at their highest level in the flower during the night, lasting until about 9:00 or 10:00 am; Young Living harvests the flowers only during the early morning hours. It is also important that the flowers used in the distillation process are of the correct growth stage. Overly ripe flowers begin to oxidize and hydrolyze, giving a faint sour note to the oil; too young flowers do not contain sufficient level of essential oil, and neither will qualify as the highest quality "fine grade". It is this knowledge that is taught to the harvesting crew that sets the Young Living Ylang Ylang grade oil apart from most commercial distillations.

CHAPTER 5

Materia Medica

We will list some of the better known, more popular oils and oil blends offered by Young Living with their benefits. This list is by no means complete and there are many uses for the oils as they are not single-faceted as are synthetic drugs. You can look up more oils and their uses on the Young Living website at http://www.youngliving.com/en_US/essential-and-massage-oils. The *Essential Oils Desk Reference* is also a valuable reference tool; please see the Recommended Resources section. The action of the oils listed below are primarily from anecdotal evidence (except where referenced) and are not to be construed as being endorsed by the FDA; it is up to the individual to make your own judgments.

> Please Note: Oils containing furanoid compounds can be phototoxic and may cause sunburn; do NOT apply these oils and allow the animal to go into sunshine for several hours afterward (these oils are best applied at night); applies to topical use only, not internal consumption. The phototoxic oils include: Angelica, Anise, Bergamot, Bitter Orange (Neroli: only ones that are expressed, not absolutes), Cumin, Fennel, Grapefruit, Lemon, Lime, Petitgrain, Rue; as well as any of the blends containing these singles. This applies whether diluted or not. (Stewart 2004, pp381-382) Also check the Desk Reference if in doubt.
>
> Do not use Fennel, Hyssop, or wild Tansy in animals that are suspected of being seizure-prone or having high blood pressure.

Single Oils

Balsam Fir, Idaho (Abies balsamea) oil is a great addition to supporting arthritis or rheumatic pain. Asthma, respiratory and skin ailments all have a relationship, so keep that in mind as you seek to assist your pet companion holistically as the whole animal he or she is.

Basil (Ocimum basilicum) is versatile and has many uses – plus it's great for cooking our human food too! Topically, Basil can help as a muscle relaxant, and reduce inflammation.

Chamomile, German (Matricaria recutita) oil can be helpful for animals that have arthritis (applied via massage or Raindrop technique), cuts, dermatitis, inflamed skin, insect bites, sores, strains, stress, wounds, muscle pain for working dogs/horses, sensitive skin.

Chamomile, Roman (Chamaemelum nobile) oil can be helpful for muscle pain, puppy teething pain, great for burns, wounds, reducing inflammation, allergic reactions, dry itchy skin, dermatitis, hypersensitive skin. Roman Chamomile essential oil is a deep cleanser of the liver. Great for canine massage!

Cedarwood, (Cedrus atlantica) helps to loosen and remove mucus during attacks of bronchitis, kennel cough and other congestive conditions; is highly effective in treating infected skin conditions and/or dandruff, insect repellent/deterrent.

Cistus (Cistus ladanifer) oil is also known as Rock Rose and has long been studied for its effect on cell regeneration. It has a very strong aroma so it's best to use diluted. It is calming to nerves and can also be simultaneously uplifting. It is also used to stop bleeding (for example, trimming a dog's nails to close).

Clary Sage (Salvia sclarea) can be helpful for animals that are nervous and stressed for various reasons.

Clove (Szygium aromaticum) oil is a wonderful, all-purpose oil; it has germicidal properties and a numbing/analgesic effect. Due to its topical antiseptic properties, clove oil is useful for ring worm, wound care, cuts, scabies and other fungal infections. It can also assist with arthritis, infections, and parasites.

Coriander (Coriandrum sativum) oil is useful for aches, arthritis, colic, gout, indigestion, nausea, rheumatism.

Cypress (Cupressus sempervirens) oil may be beneficial for asthma, strengthening connective tissue, intestinal parasites, pancreas insufficiencies and pulmonary infections; it may also help to improve circulation thus aiding in resorption of bruises. It is also listed as a haemostatic (stops bleeding) and a hepatic (liver protectant). Jean Valnet, M.D. suggests that it may be helpful for some cancers (Valnet and Tisserand 1982, p120).

Eucalyptus (Eucalyptus globulus) is an oil that can be used for respiratory issues, wounds, inflammations, cuts, muscle aches and may relieve some pain; it can repel/deter insects.

Frankincense (Boswellia carteri) may help with wound healing, sores, bug bites, immune enhancing. There have also been a number of recent university studies showing the medicinal benefits of Frankincense for issues such as arthritis, anxiety and even cancer; it may shrink and dissolve fatty tumors.

Galbanum (Ferula gummosa) oil is great oil for balancing, increasing in frequency when used with Frankincense or Sandalwood. It assists with digestive and skin issues. Because it has analgesic properties it can be helpful in assisting with arthritis or other similar issues.

Geranium (Pelargonium graveolens) is great for skin problems, balances the emotions and a great insect repellent/deterrent - especially against ticks!

Ginger (Zingiber officinale) oil eases nausea, use as a digestive aid; assists with motion sickness,; is good for easing arthritis, and respiratory issues.

Grapefruit (Citrus x paradisi) may help coat and skin care, great for smelly, oily coats and has quite a happy aroma. Grapefruit oil can help as support for depression, obesity, liver disorders, anxiety, and tumor growth.

Helichrysum (Helichrysum italicum) oil seems to help heal most cuts, hot spots, dermatitis, irritated skin, and minor wounds. It can prevent the formation of scar tissue or even help resolve old scar tissue, regenerate nerves, and chelates toxins and chemicals from the liver.

Hyssop (H. officinalis) can be great for skin problems. It can be used for paw sores and hot spots. Hyssop can prevent the pathogenic bacterial build up in wounds, and can help with fungal infections. It contains astringent properties that help to reduce swelling by constricting blood vessels, and may help to slow excessive bleeding. When applied to arthritic joints, it reduces swelling and pain by helping to improve circulation through those areas. ***Caution: do not use Hyssop in dogs with seizures.***

Jasmine Absolute (Jasminum officinale) can help your animal (or yourself) have a better and more sound sleep even when suffering from respiratory conditions. It gives relief from coughing by helping clear the accumulation of phlegm in the respiratory tracts. Also, being a cicatrisant, it can help fade away scar marks. A natural sedative, it calms down body, mind and emotions and brings forth positive and happier emotions. It gives relief from anxiety, stress, annoyance, anger and depression as well as reduces inflammation in the body.

Juniper (Juniperus osteosperma and/or J. scopulorum) properties are almost endless, another wonderful oil to keep on hand. It efficiently protects wounds from becoming septic. It promotes and improves circulation. It helps in the removal of toxins such as uric acid from the body so it helps fight ailments like arthritis, renal calculi etc., which are related to improper circulation. Juniper is effective on almost all forms of cramps, be it muscular, intestinal, or respiratory. A natural carminative, it helps with the removal of gases from the intestines. It increases frequency of urination, thus, it is very beneficial for animals who are suffering from accumulation of fluids or water in the body, swelling, etc., due to chronic renal failure. Juniper cleans blood of toxins and thus acts as a blood purifier. It helps remove toxins like heavy metals, pollutants and certain compounds produced by the body itself, as well as other foreign toxins which get into the blood. Juniper oil may help in dissolving kidney stones, with urinary tract infections and skin diseases. Juniper oil is a wonderful, general tonic because it tones up everything, including muscles, tissues, skin, as well as various systems functioning inside the body, such as the respiratory system, circulatory system, nervous system, digestive system and the excretory system. This tonic effect helps maintain proper balance and hence good health.

Lavender (Lavandula agustifolia) is yet another oil with so many uses and benefits. Lavender can act as "anti-histamine" and may help with allergies. It can be used for sores, cuts, dermatitis, insect bites, bruises, itching, teeth cleaning, and as a great bug deterrent. It is excellent for soothing any sort of skin condition or bug bites. Lavender essential oil has a calming scent which makes it an excellent tonic for the nerves, and therefore helps in assisting with anxiety, depression, nervous tension, emotional stress, nervous exhaustion, and restlessness. Lavender essential oil is also an excellent remedy for various types of pains such as sore tense muscles, muscular aches, sprains and arthritis. A regular massage with lavender oil may provide relief from pain in the joints. Lavender essential oil is also good for urinary disorders as it stimulates urine production. It helps in restoring hormonal balance and reduces cystitis or inflammation of the bladder. Lavender is good for improving blood circulation in the body. Lavender oil is useful for digestion as it increases the motility of the intestine. The oil also stimulates the production of gastric juices and bile and thus aids in treating indigestion, stomach pain, colic, vomiting and diarrhea. And the regular use of lavender oil - like most medical grade oils - builds immunity as it provides resistance to disease conditions.

Lemon (Citrus limon) oil stimulates white blood cells and thus increases the ability to thwart disease conditions. Lemon oil may help improve the circulation in the body. It is good for some infections as it has antiseptic properties, reduces inflammation, and is a good digestive aid and liver cleanser. When diffused it helps to lift the spirits, dispel depression and anxiety. With its topical antiseptic properties, lemon oil is commonly used as cleansing agent in place of toxic, chemical-based cleaners.

Laurus Nobilis (L. nobilis) oil is better known as bay laurel. It is used for a wide variety of things including but not limited to nerve regeneration, convulsions, viral, yeast and respiratory conditions, etc.

Marjoram (Origanum majorana) oil has a warming action; it calms emotions, relieves anxiety as well as stress and helps to calms hyperactive animals. It may help ease nervous reactions before transportation, vet visits, during thunder storms, etc. It has muscle relaxant properties and the pain reducing properties are useful for arthritic pain as well as sprains, strains and spasms, swollen joints and painful muscles. Marjoram oil soothes the digestive system and helps with indigestion, constipation and flatulence, and has a beneficial action on the respiratory system.

Melissa (Melissa officinalis) is considered one of the most powerful medicinal essential oils in all of aromatherapy. To quote Kurt Schnaubelt: "The way in which melissa oil combines an excellent antiviral component with a soothing but pervasive sedative power is difficult to imagine; it has to be experienced. In its complexity, power, and gentleness, melissa oil perfectly illustrates how nature time after time works better than one-dimensional synthetic medicines." (Schnaubelt 1998, p80) Melissa is a strong, powerful immune enhancer; in particular it supports the body against pathogenic viral stages, including the ability to resolve herpes outbreak via topical application. (Schnaubelt 1998, p80), (Schnitzler *et al.* 2008) It may be possible to also deactivate viruses such as parvovirus and distemper, among others.

Myrrh (Commiphora myrrha) bestows benefits that are immune enhancing, astringent, topical antiseptic, antimicrobial, natural fungicide and pesticide; it may deactivate viruses, may be a cellular rejuvenator, expectorant and sedative. It may aid in healing skin rashes, hot spots, minor wounds, ear and teeth care. Fleas and ticks seem to dislike the odor.

Myrtle (Myrtus communis) oil is largely used for its topical antiseptic properties; however, Myrtle essential oil is also astringent, antimicrobial, expectorant, toning and uplifting emotionally. It can assist with bruising, respiratory issues, skin issues, prostate problems, thyroid problems, and muscle spasms. The ancient Greeks used it for bladder and lung infections. It has also been researched for its effects in normalizing hormonal imbalances.

Nutmeg (Myristica fragrans) stimulates the heart and circulation and activates the mind while stimulating the digestive system and aids with gas, nausea, chronic vomiting and diarrhea. It encourages appetite and averts constipation, fights gallstones and encourages appetite. The oil has shown to be good at reducing inflammation as well as successful in relieving muscular aches and pain, as well as arthritis.

Oregano (Thymus capitus) benefits can be attributed to its properties that enhance the immune system, protect against harmful stages of pathogens and parasites, reduce inflammation; it has antioxidant properties, aids digestion, as well as can reduce symptoms of allergies. The disinfectant and bactericide properties of this oil were recognized in ancient Greece where they used for treating bacterial infections on skin wounds and also to protect food stuff from bacteria. New research is discovering that Oregano may inhibit the growth of cancer cells, and can clear up some infections related to herpes. It is also used as an insect repellent diluted or added to other essential oils before applied to the skin. Please note this is a "HOT" oil and best used diluted with animals.

Palo Santo (Bursera graveolens) is in the same family as Frankincense and is sometimes referred to as "South American Frankincense". It is highly regarded as a spiritual oil. Attributes of physical healing may include joint and tendon/ligament conditions, broken bones, fungal infections and other skin conditions; it is reputedly good for "tired feet" – (or hooves and paws).

Peppermint (Mentha piperita) can protect the body from harmful bacteria or rather change the frequency of the harmful bacteria allowing the body to come back into a healthy balance. A 2010 study in "Pharmacognosy Magazine" revealed that the flavonoids in Peppermint oil are potent antimicrobials. (Sharafi *et al.* 2010) This study showed that Peppermint oil has bactericidal properties for E. coli, Staphylococcus, Pseudomonas, and others. A 2010 report in "Journal of Cancer Research and Therapeutics" demonstrated that Peppermint leaf extract reduced tissue damage caused by radiation therapy in animal studies. The radioprotective effects appeared to be due to antioxidant and free radical-scavenging properties afforded by Peppermint's flavonoids, which are present in both its extracts and its essential oil. (Baliga and Rao 2010) Soothing to the intestine, Peppermint oil is effective for colic-like symptoms as well as Irritable Bowel Syndrome. (Balch 2002, pp108-109) This multi-faceted oil may also repel insects and fleas. It also seems to have a cooling effect on itchy canine or equine skin. You can remove ticks by applying a drop of Peppermint oil on a cotton swab and swabbing the tick; wait for it to unhinge its head and remove from your animal.

Rose (Rosa damascena) has one of the highest frequencies – 320 MHz – to date, surpassed only by Idaho Blue Spruce; it is a highly prized oil with many health encouraging properties physically and emotionally! Rose oil can boost self-esteem, confidence, hope and mental strength; it can be very helpful to relieve symptoms of depression from animals (including humans). It may help calm down a high fever by sedating the inflammation in the body. It can also be beneficial in other cases of inflammations caused by microbes, ingestion of poisonous items, indigestion, dehydration etc. This fragrant oil also has topical antiseptic and bactericidal properties, and it can efficiently relieve spasms in the respiratory system, intestines and muscular spasms in limbs. It also may alleviate convulsions, muscle pulls, cramps and spasmodic cholera which are caused due to spasms.

Rosemary (Rosmarinus officinalis CT 1,8 cineol) oil can be good for healing of wounds and improve a dull-looking coat. Generally used for dandruff and seborrhea.

Rosewood (Aniba rosaeordora) is wonderful for skin issues, and is also empowering and emotionally stabilizing. It assists in fungal issues in the skin and can also improve the skin's elasticity. (Please note, it may not be available as a single oil at this time, only in blends.)

Sandalwood (Santalum album) is an oil good for the skin. It can help with sleep issues and is found in a variety of the Young Living blends.

Thyme (Thymus vulgaris CT thymol) works on canine/equine eczema, and staph infections, as well as another great deterrent against parasites.

Ylang Ylang (Cananga odorata) can reduce tachycardia (fast heart beat) and tachypnea (fast, shallow breathing) due to its calming abilities. Anxiety, high blood pressure and tension are also positively affected with just a drop or two. Used in massage therapy, it will help to relax muscles and alleviate muscle spasms. Also under the "calming" umbrella, inflammatory skin conditions such as dermatitis, eczema and other skin conditions may be relieved with the use of Ylang Ylang.

Blends and Recipes

When you blend essential oils together, the chemical constituents in individual oils can have a mutually enhancing synergetic effect on the others. This working together of two or more essential oils results in an effect greater – or perhaps different – than the sum of their individual effects. More powerful therapeutic results are often obtained when certain essential oils are blended together than when used individually.

There is both a science and art to creating your own blends. Since this book is intended primarily as a naturopathic overview, we will not go into detail, but wanted you to be aware that thinking "outside the box" would be of great benefit here, and the "no fear factor" definitely applies! The worst you can do in creating your own blend is to create something less effective than it could be otherwise. A couple of good resources to begin with are: *The Chemistry of Essential Oils Made Simple* by David Stewart (pp112-114) and *Advanced Aromatherapy* by Kurt Schnaubelt (pp57-58)

Below are just a few of the many wonderful synergetic blends made by Young Living – please refer to the *Essential Oils Desk Reference* for a complete listing (see Recommended Resources section). Following that we have included some recipes for blends.

Aroma Life can bring vitality to the heart and overall circulation: Cypress (Cupressus sempervirens), Marjoram (Origanum majorana), Helichrysum (Helichrysum italicum), and Ylang Ylang (Cananga odorata) in a base of sesame seed oil.

Aroma Siez is used to help ease pain and to relax muscles stressed from exercise: Basil (Ocimum basilicum), Marjoram (Origanum majorana), Lavender (Lavandula angustifolia), Peppermint (Mentha piperita), and Cypress (Cupressus sempervirens).

Brain Power is one that is indicated for problems such as brain damage, cognitive dysfunction (animals are now presenting with autistic like symptoms), neurologic disorders, and obsessive behaviors: Frankincense, Sandalwood, Melissa, Cedarwood, Blue Cypress, Lavender, and Helichrysum.

Common Sense blend is indicated and can assist with problems with the brain and can help with increasing brain function, anxiety, neurologic conditions, seizures, increasing learning ability, brain damage: Frankincense, Ylang Ylang, Ocotea, Ruta, Dorado Azul, and Lime.

EndoFlex is a blend that may help overall vitality. It contains oils that are associated with glandular balance: Spearmint (Mentha spicata), Sage (Salvia officinalis), Geranium (Pelargonium graveolens), Myrtle (Myrtus communis), Nutmeg (Myristica fragrans), and German Chamomile (Matricaria recutita) in a base of sesame seed oil.

ImmuPower blend was specifically created for building, strengthening, and protecting the body: Cistus (Cistus ladanifer), Frankincense (Boswellia carteri), Hyssop (Hyssopus officinalis), Ravintsara (Cinnamomum camphora), Mountain Savory (Satureja montana), Oregano (Origanum compactum), Clove (Syzygium aromaticum), Cumin (Cuminum cyminum), and Idaho Tansy (Tanacetum vulgare). **Caution: do not use Hyssop in dogs with seizures.**

JuvaFlex is a combination of oils that have been studied for their supportive and clearing effects on the liver and digestion: Fennel (Foeniculum vulgare), Geranium (Pelargonium graveolens), Rosemary (Rosmarinus officinalis), Roman Chamomile (Chamaemelum nobile), Blue Tansy (Tanacetum annuum), and Helichrysum (Helichrysum italicum) in a base of sesame seed oil.

Healing Recipes with Essential Oils

The following recipes were once proprietary to Dr. Kim Bloomer's Aspenbloom Pet Care. Since she discontinued the line to focus solely on promoting the actual essential oils themselves, she wanted to make these three recipes available to the public.

The sprays were "Be Calm" for calming, "Be Free" for pest control and "Be Soothed" for skin issues. All were available in 4 oz glass bottles only.

Be Calm Recipe

3 drops each of the following EOs: Cistus, Cedarwood, Cypress, Frankincense, Galbanum, Myrrh and Spikenard

2 drops of Roman Chamomile

1 drop of Lavender

2-3 drops of Animal Scents shampoo as an emulsifier

Fill bottle with Lemon Balm hydrosol water (certified organic such as from Mountain Rose Herbs)

Be Free Recipe

5 drops each of the following EOs: Cassia, Cedarwood, Hyssop, Myrrh

Caution: do not use Hyssop in dogs with seizures.

3 drops each of the following EOs: Lemongrass, Geranium, Rosemary

1 drop Lavender

2-3 drops of Animal Scents shampoo as an emulsifier

Fill bottle with Rose Geranium or Peppermint hydrosol water (certified organic such as from Mountain Rose Herbs)

Be Soothed Recipe

2 drops each of the following EOs: Cedarwood, Cypress, Frankincense, Galbanum, Hyssop, Myrtle, Myrrh, Spikenard

Caution: do not use Hyssop in dogs with seizures.

2 drops of Lavender

1 drop of Roman Chamomile

A few drops of Grapefruit seed extract (organic from Mountain Rose Herbs)

2-3 drops of Animal Scents shampoo as an emulsifier

Fill bottle with Rose Cucumber or Lavender hydrosol water (certified organic only such as from Mountain Rose Herbs)

Transformation

CHAPTER 6

The Future of Animal Aromatherapy

Even though this book is technically an "introduction" into the use of essential oils with animals, we hesitated calling it that as we feel it addresses some aspects within the natural health field that are not generally recognized. Each of us that contributed to this book has had the privilege of knowing great animal teachers; their messages are an intricate part of our work. We each continue on our own learning path, converging to help advance the knowledge of true holistic animal health.

We hope this book has both helped you overcome any fears you may have as well as stimulated your interest to delve deeper into many of the aspects that have been presented here. The authors of this book see the use of essential oils with animals evolving out of a materialistic, allopathic-drug-replacement methodology, transforming into a cohesive, interactive communication between human and non-human. As we bring the ancient traditions of natural healing into the future with higher, more spiritual intent and knowing, we will be able to weave a thread between us and animals in which they become co-facilitators in their own healing and sustainability, leading us humans to a greater understanding of their needs. Is this too much of a dream? We think not. We have for too long continued down a path of domination, reductionism, and mechanism over nature, including our companion animals. We truly feel humanity is poised to transcend this. To that end, whatever small part we, the authors of this book, play in this transformation, we are honored to do so. We sincerely hope you, the reader, will join us on a wonderful journey.

> "We need another and a wiser and perhaps a more mystical concept of animals. Remote from universal nature and living by complicated artifice, man in civilization surveys the creature through the glass of his knowledge and sees thereby a feather magnified and the whole image in distortion. We patronize them for their incompleteness, for their tragic fate for having taken form so far below ourselves. And therein do we err. For the animal shall not be measured by man. In a world older and more complete than ours, they move finished and complete, gifted with the extension of the senses we have lost or never attained, living by voices we shall never hear. They are not brethren, they are not underlings: they are other nations, caught with ourselves in the net of life and time, fellow prisoners of the splendour and travail of the earth." Henry Beston, The Outermost House, 1928

Recommended Resources

Most of these can be found on Amazon; the Desk References are best purchased through Life Science Publishing (http://www.lifesciencepublishers.com/).

Desk References
Essential Oils Desk Reference, by Gary Young, Young Living, various

Reference Guide for Essential Oils, by Connie & Alan Higley

Other Books/Booklets
The Healing Power of Essential Oils, by Rodolphe Balz

(Please note this book (Balz) is based on the British School of administering essential oil, however does contain some very decent information otherwise.)

The Body Electric, by Robert O. Becker

Transcendental Physics, by Edward R. Close

The Cognitive Horse, by Francesco De Giorgio and José Schoorl

Essential Oils 101, by Carrie Donegan & Elena Yordán

Messages from the Water, by Masaru Emoto

Wild Health: Lessons in Natural Wellness from the Animal Kingdom, by Cindy Engel

The Art, Science and Business of Aromatherapy, By Kayla Fioravanti

The Nature of Substance, by Rudolf Hauschka

Aromatherapy for Horses, by Caroline Ingraham

The Inner Carnivore, by Jennifer Lee

The Biology of Belief, by Bruce H. Lipton

Releasing Emotional Patterns with Essential Oils, by Carolyn L. Mein

Dogs: Their True Origin, Function, and Future, by Aleksandra Mikic

Molecules of Emotion, by Candace Pert

Equine Nutrition: from a Species Appropriate Perspective, by Sarah Reagan

Advanced Aromatherapy, by Kurt Schnaubelt

Medical Aromatherapy: Healing with Essential Oils, by Kurt Schnaubelt

The Healing Intelligence of Essential Oils, by Kurt Schnaubelt

The Ion Effect, by Fred Soyka with Alan Edmond

Healing Oils of the Bible, by David Stewart

Quantum Physics, Essential Oils, and the Mind-Body Connection (booklet), by David Stewart (see Life Science Publishing)

The Chemistry of Essential Oils Made Simple, by David Stewart

The Secret Life of Plants, by Peter Tompkins and Christopher Bird

The Practice of Aromatherapy, by Jean Valnet

The Dynamic Legacy: from Homeopathy to Heilkunst, by Rudi Verspoor and Steven Decker

(available here: http://www.heilkunst.com/table.html#book2)

Equine Acupressure: A Working Manual, by Nancy Zidonis, Amy Snow, Marie Soderberg

Web Articles

Raindrop Messenger Archive – many good articles by Dr. David Stewart

(including the one on Quantum Physics and Essential Oils referenced in fn 7)

http://www.raindroptraining.com/messenger/article_index.shtml

Coursework

American Council of Animal Naturopathy

PO Box 15505

Rio Rancho, NM 87174-5505

505-715-6617

http://www.animalnaturopathy.org/

Young Living Essential Oils & Supplements

To purchase any of the Young Living essential oils and products you will need to sign up through an existing Young Living distributor at either a retail or wholesale (distributor) level. Distributors receive a substantial discount on all Young Living essential oils and products; have access to sales and special offers, as well as the ability to earn free products every month through the Essential Rewards Program. Retail customers buy products at full retail pricing. You are not under any obligation to sell the oils and products at any time or make it a business unless you want to.

Dr. Kim Bloomer

Sponsor/Enroller ID# 767865

Website: http://www.aspenbloom.com

Dr. Jeannie (Jeanette) Thomason

Sponsor/Enroller # 719671

Website: http://www.aromanotes.com/drjeannie

Dr. Sarah Reagan

Sponsor/Enroller ID# 1172613

Website: http://ylwebsite.com/learningoils/

Animal Chakra Charts

The following charts, photo(s), and content are from the website of www.patinkas.co.uk and are for informational purposes only. They are used with permission as stated on the website.

Copyright image provided courtesy of Patinkas © 2009-2012.

Copyright text excerpt provided courtesy of Patinkas © 2009-2012.

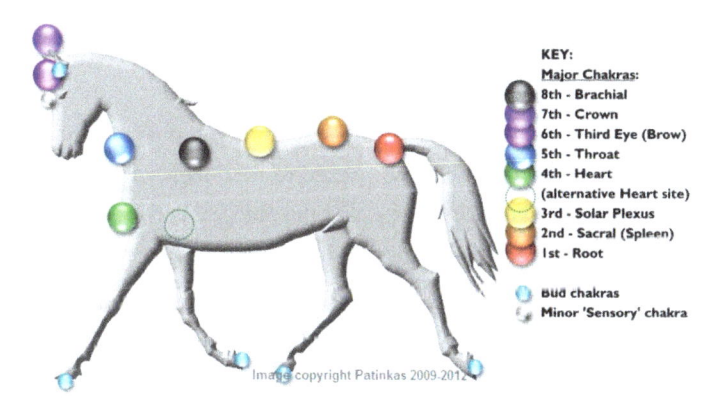

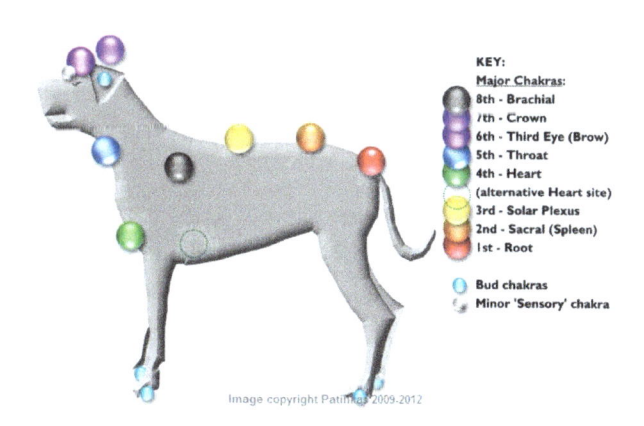

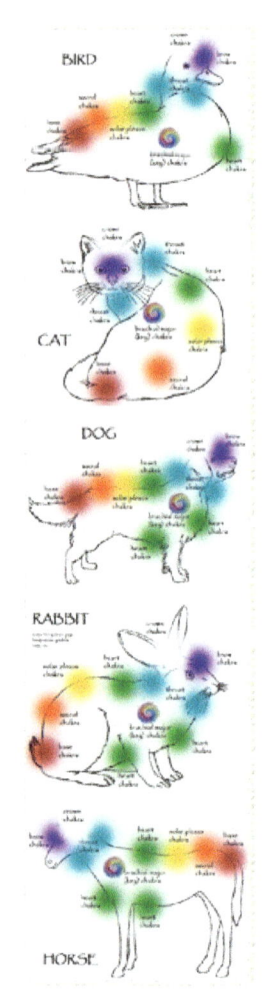

Animals, in common with all other living beings, have a chakra system. This system is a complex network of spinning, energy vortices (often called 'petals' in Eastern traditions) which run throughout the entire body. Universal energy (Prana, Chi, Ki) flows in and out of the chakras, along the meridian system, into the aura and then finally into the physical body. The energy flows two ways; inward and out. Therefore, every thought, act and emotion affects the chakras and is mirrored in the aura. Likewise, external stimuli, both positive and negative, have an effect on the chakras and leave their mark in the aura (including physical injuries). This is the same for animals and humans alike.

For those unfamiliar with the chakra system, if you imagine the subtle energy body (made up of chakras, linked to meridians and contained in the aura) as being like a car engine, and the physical body is the actual vehicle which the engine drives, it is not difficult to see that when the car starts to perform less effectively or even breaks down, that it's the engine which needs repairing or re-tuning and not the car bodywork. It's the same with the subtle energy body. When we re-charge/realign the chakras - get them spinning in harmony and at the correct rate – you get the physical body running smoothly once again.

Animal Chakras

Animals have 8 Major chakras, 21 Minor chakras and 6 Bud chakras. Alongside the seven Major chakras that animals share with humans (Crown, Third Eye, Throat, Heart, Solar Plexus, Sacral and Root), there is another Major chakra which is unique to animals. It is called the Brachial or Key chakra. This chakra was discovered by the world's foremost, internationally renowned, animal healer, Margrit Coates.

Frequencies of Essential Oils

The following chart information is from the Young Living *Essential Oils Desk Reference*, 5th Ed. Since that book was written, it has been determined the Idaho Blue Spruce has the highest frequency so far at 580 MHz, which is higher than Rose oil.

Frequencies of Single Essential Oils and Blends

SINGLE ESSENTIAL OILS

Oil	Frequency
Angelica	85 MHz
Basil	52 MHz
Frankincense	147 MHz
Galbanum	56 MHz
German Chamomile	105 MHz
Helichrysum	181 MHz
Idaho Tansy	105 MHz
Juniper	98 MHz
Lavender	118 MHz
Melissa (lemon balm)	102 MHz
Myrrh	105 MHz
Peppermint	78 MHz
Ravintsara	134 MHz
Rose	320 MHz
Sandalwood	96 MHz

ESSENTIAL OIL BLENDS

Abundance	78 MHz
Acceptance	102 MHz
Aroma Life	84 MHz
Aroma Siez	64 MHz
Awaken	89 MHz
Brain Power	78 MHz
Christmas Spirit	104 MHz
Citrus Fresh	90 MHz
Clarity	101 MHz
Di-Tone	102 MHz
Dragon Time	72 MHz
Dream Catcher	98 MHz
EndoFlex	138 MHz
En-R-Gee	106 MHz
Envision	90 MHz
Exodus II	180 MHz
Forgiveness	192 MHz
Gathering	99 MHz
Gentle Baby	152 MHz
Grounding	140 MHz
Harmony	101 MHz
Hope	98 MHz
Humility	88 MHz
ImmuPower	89 MHz
Inner Child	98 MHz
Inspiration	141 MHz
Into the Future	88 MHz
Joy	188 MHz
Juva Flex	82 MHz
Live With Passion	89 MHz
Magnify Your Purpose	99 MHz
Melrose	48 MHz
Mister	147 MHz
Motivation	103 MHz
M-Grain	72 MHz
PanAway	112 MHz
Peace & Calming	105 MHz
Present Time	98 MHz
Purification	46 MHz
Raven	70 MHz
R.C.	75 MHz
Release	102 MHz
Relieve It	56 MHz
Sacred Mountain	176 MHz
SARA	102 MHz
Sensation	88 MHz
Surrender	98 MHz
Thieves	150 MHz
3 Wise Men	72 MHz
Trauma Life	92 MHz
Valor	47 MHz
White Angelica	89 MHz

Bibliography

Aga, M., *et al.*, 2001. Preventive effect of Coriandrum sativum (Chinese parsley) on localized lead deposition in ICR mice. *Journal of Ethnopharmacology* [online], 77 (2–3), 203–208. Available from: http://www.sciencedirect.com/science/article/pii/S0378874101002999 [Accessed 12 Jun 2014].

Balch, P.A., 2002. *Prescription for herbal healing.* New York: Avery.

Baliga, M.S. and Rao, S., 2010. Radioprotective potential of mint: a brief review. *Journal of cancer research and therapeutics*, 6 (3), 255–262.

Balz, R., Dandrieux, B., and Lartaud, P., 1999. *The healing power of essential oils: Fragrance secrets for everyday use.* 1st ed. Delhi: Motilal Banarsidass.

Bortoft, H., 1996. *The wholeness of nature: Goethe's way toward a science of conscious participation in nature.* Hudson, NY: Lindisfarne Press.

Fioravanti, K., 2011. *Art, science and business of aromatherapy: Your guide for personal aromatherapy ...* [S.l.]: Selah Press.

Hardy, M., n.d. *Anthroposophic medicine the logical way to approach essential oils in a spiritual fashion* [online]. Allegan MI. Available from: http://www.templeofsakkara.com/anthropos.htm [Accessed 22 Apr 2014].

K. Husnu Can Baser, Gerhard Buchbauer, ed., 2010. *Handbook of essential oils: science, technology, and applications.* Boca Raton FL: CRC Press, Taylor & Francis Group.

Lipton, B.H., 2008. *The biology of belief: Unleashing the power of consciousness, matter & miracles.* Carlsbad, Calif: Hay House.

Samojlik, I., *et al.*, 2010. Antioxidant and hepatoprotective potential of essential oils of coriander (Coriandrum sativum L.) and caraway (Carum carvi L.) (Apiaceae). *Journal of agricultural and food chemistry*, 58 (15), 8848–8853.

Schad, W., 1977. *Man and mammals: Toward a biology of form.* Garden City, N.Y: Waldorf Press.

Schnaubelt, K., 1998. *Advanced aromatherapy: The science of essential oil therapy.* 1st ed. Rochester, Vt: Healing Arts Press.

Schnaubelt, K., 1999. *Medical aromatherapy: Healing with essential oils.* Berkeley, Calif: Frog.

Schnitzler, P., *et al.*, 2008. Melissa officinalis oil affects infectivity of enveloped herpesviruses. *Phytomedicine : international journal of phytotherapy and phytopharmacology*, 15 (9), 734–740.

Sell, C., 2010. Chemistry of essential oils. *In:* K. Husnu Can Baser, Gerhard Buchbauer, ed. *Handbook of essential oils: science, technology, and applications.* Boca Raton FL: CRC Press, Taylor & Francis Group, 121.

Sharafi, S.M., *et al.*, 2010. Protective effects of bioactive phytochemicals from Mentha piperita with multiple health potentials. *Pharmacognosy magazine* [online], 6 (23), 147–153. Available from: http://www.phcog.com/article.asp?issn=0973-1296;year=2010;volume=6;issue=23;spage=147;epage=153;aulast=Sharafi [Accessed 7 Jun 2014].

Soyka, F., 1971, 1977. *The ion effect.* Minneapolis MN: Bantam Books.

Stewart, D., ©2002. *Healing oils of the Bible.* 1st ed. Marble Hill, MO: Center for Aromatherapy Research & Education.

Stewart, D., 2003. The blood-brain barrier. *The Raindrop Messenger* [online], 1 (1). Available from: http://www.raindroptraining.com/messenger/v1n1.html#one [Accessed 10 Jun 2014].

Stewart, D., 2004. *The chemistry of essential oils made simple: God's love manifest in molecules.* 1st ed. Marble Hill, Mo: Care Publications.

Stewart, D., 2009. Quantum physics, essential oils & the mind-body connection. *The Raindrop Messenger* [online], 7 (1). Available from: http://www.raindroptraining.com/messenger/v7n1.html#quantum [Accessed 7 May 2014].

Stewart, D., 2011. Do essential oils contain proteins, enzymes, vitamins, or hormones? *The Raindrop Messenger* [online], 9 (5). Available from: http://www.raindroptraining.com/messenger/v9n5.html#enzymes [Accessed 5 May 2014].

Strachan, D. and Karnstedt, J., n.d. *Negative ions - vitamins of the air* [online]. Available from: http://www.negativeionsinformation.org/ions_vitamins.html [Accessed 26 Apr 2014].

Valnet, J. and Tisserand, R., 1982. *The practice of aromatherapy.* Saffron Walden: Daniel.

Verspoor, R. and Decker, S., 2000. *The dynamic legacy: hahnemann from homeopathy to heilkunst: Book II: Therapeutic regimen.* Manotick ON: Hahnemann Center for Heilkunst.

Zidonis, N.A., Soderberg, M.K., and Snow, A., 2001. *Equine acupressure: A working manual.* 4th ed. Larkspur, Colo: Tallgrass Publishers.

Authors

Dr. Sarah Reagan

is a Certified Animal Naturopath, holds the Advanced Diploma in Veterinary Homeopathy, and is currently working toward a degree in Human/Animal Studies. Her area of expertise is horses and cats in all aspects, including species appropriate nutrition, behavior, homeopathy, and aromatherapy. Dr. Sarah writes and consults; teaches the equine courses at the American Council of Animal Naturopathy (ACAN). She continues to pursue studies in Goethean/Holistic Science. She is also the author of *Equine Nutrition: From a Species Appropriate Perspective*, available on Amazon. Her website/blog is http://ahorsesview.com/.

Dr. Kim Bloomer

is a Certified Animal Naturopath and published author, consulting on canine and feline nutrition and wellness. She is the Co-Founder of the American Council of Animal Naturopathy. In addition, Dr. Kim is a proficient blogger and writer on natural pet health, having co-authored the book, *Whole Health for Happy Dogs* and authored the book *Animals Taught Me That*. Dr. Kim's articles have been featured in various publications such as Animal Wellness, Natural Horse, Dogs Naturally, NM Breeze, Raw Instincts, and the Pet Connection Canada. Her website is www.AspenbloomPetCare.com.

Dr. Jeannie Thomason

is a Certified Animal Naturopath, offering consultations in canine, feline and avian nutrition & aromatherapy. She is the Founder of the Natural Rearing Breeders Association and Co-Founder of the American Council of Animal Naturopathy as well as a prolific article writer whose articles have been featured in Raw Instincts, Pet Connection Canada, Dogs Naturally, Animal Wellness Magazine, Bella Dog, Natural Horse, and several national breed magazines. Her website is http://www.thewholedog.org.

CPSIA information can be obtained at www.ICGtesting.com
Printed in the USA
LVOW02s1941290315

432407LV00001B/1/P